The Ageless Orgasm: Secrets to a Steamy Second Chapter [Great Sex Life for The 40+]

By

Alton C. Raymond

About the Author

The prolific content writer Alton C. Raymond has extensive knowledge of intimate and sexual topics. Alton dives into many parts of sexual wellness to provide helpful insights and counselling, drawing on a lifelong interest in the complexities of human connection. His art is an attempt to normalise candid discussions about sexuality and to dismantle social taboos around the subject. With his captivating material and kind demeanour, Alton demonstrates his commitment to helping individuals and couples live satisfying and enjoyable lives.

Table of Contents

Introduction:

Welcome to "The Ageless Orgasm: Secrets to a Steamy Second Chapter." This book is your guide to finding pleasure, sensuality, and breaking free from what society says about sex when you reach your 40s and beyond.

This manual is aimed to enable persons aged 40 and beyond to accept and enhance their sexual experiences. With an emphasis on reigniting desire, overcoming age-related hurdles, and cultivating closeness, this book attempts to give practical guidance, techniques, and insights to help readers have full and gratifying sex lives in their "second chapter" of life.

Life really may feel like a whirlwind sometimes, especially when we balance job, family, and everything in between. But here's the thing: our love life doesn't have to take a backseat simply because we're getting older. In fact, now is the best time to rekindle that spark and make our love life even better than before.

Embracing your sexuality in midlife is all about feeling comfortable and satisfied with your sexual self as you become older.

So, assume you're in your 40s or beyond, and you're starting to notice some changes in how you feel about sex. Maybe you're not as interested as you used to be, or maybe you're inquisitive about trying new things. That's absolutely typical!

It's like this: Your body and your feelings about sex might change as you get older, and that's alright. Embracing your sexuality involves embracing those changes and figuring out what makes you feel comfortable and joyful.

It's not just about tangible goods either. It's also about connecting with yourself and your spouse (if you have one) on a deeper level. Maybe that means having honest talks about what you want and need, or maybe it involves finding new methods to feel pleasure and closeness.

And remember, there's no right or wrong way to do it. Whether you're single, in a relationship, or somewhere in between, the most essential thing is to remain loyal to yourself and do what feels right for you.

So, if you're feeling a bit hesitant or interested about your sexuality around midlife, that's entirely acceptable. Take your time, be gentle to yourself, and remember that it's all about finding joy and fulfilment in your own manner.

Are you in your 40s or beyond, and you're wondering about sex. Maybe you're asking, "Is it still a big deal at this age?" Well, let me tell you, it certainly is!

Here's why: Great sex isn't just about the physical act itself (although that's absolutely part of it). It's also about feeling connected, satisfied, and joyful, and that's something that's vital at any age, especially as we become older.

Think at it like this: As we age, our bodies change, and so do our desires and priorities. But just because we're getting older doesn't mean we have to settle for less in the bedroom. In reality, many individuals discover that their sex lives actually improve as they get older because they have more experience, confidence, and a greater awareness of what they want and need.

But here's the thing: Great sex isn't just about feeling fantastic in the moment. It can also offer some pretty fantastic long-term advantages for your health and well-being. Studies have shown that frequent, pleasant sex may help alleviate stress, enhance sleep, promote immunity, and even lessen the risk of heart disease. Plus, it's a terrific way to bond with your spouse and feel closer to them.

And the greatest part? You're never too old to have wonderful sex. Whether you're in your 40s, 50s, 60s, or beyond, there's no expiration date on pleasure. So why not embrace it and make the most of it?

So, whether you're in your 40s or beyond, remember this: Great sex is vital because it feels fantastic, enhances your relationship with your spouse, and may have all sorts of awesome advantages for your health and well-being. So go ahead, indulge in some timeless pleasure—you deserve it!

The value of wonderful sex, particularly for individuals above 40 is simply stated below:

1. Physical Health Benefits: Great sex isn't just pleasure; it's also beneficial for your body, especially as you become older. Regular sexual activity can help maintain your heart healthy by boosting blood circulation and reducing blood pressure. It also releases feel-good chemicals like endorphins, which can relieve stress and

increase your mood. Plus, it's a sort of exercise that may help keep you healthy and active.

2. Emotional Well-being: Sex isn't only a physical act—it's also a great method to connect emotionally with your spouse. As we age, keeping that emotional connection becomes even more crucial. Great sex may help build your link with your spouse, promote emotions of intimacy and closeness, and even improve communication and trust in your relationship.

3. Self-Confidence and Body Image: As we get older, our bodies unavoidably change, and sometimes that might impact how we feel about ourselves. But wonderful sex may actually help raise your self-confidence and improve your body image. Feeling wanted and fulfilled may make you feel more beautiful and confident in yourself, regardless of your age or looks.

4. Sense of Identity and Fulfilment: Sexuality is a vital element of who we are as individuals, and embracing our sexuality may make us feel more happy and alive. As we age, it's easy to get caught up in other elements of life—work, family, responsibilities—but wonderful sex reminds us that we're still lively, sensuous humans with desires and needs that need to be addressed.

5. Quality of Life: Ultimately, wonderful sex can lead to a greater overall quality of life as we age. It adds joy, pleasure, and excitement into our lives, making each day a bit brighter and more delightful. Plus, it can help us stay connected to our spouses, keep a sense of energy and youthfulness, and approach life with a more optimistic perspective.

So, if you're in your 40s or beyond, remember that amazing sex isn't just a luxury—it's a crucial element of a healthy, happy existence. Embrace your sexuality, emphasise connection with your partner, and enjoy the numerous physical, emotional, and psychological advantages that come with it.

Sometimes persons in their midlife are dragged down by baseless age-related misconceptions about sexuality that are seldom real.
By confronting these age-related beliefs about sexuality, we may encourage a more inclusive and accepting view of sexual expression at every stage of life.

Let's embrace variety, celebrate uniqueness, and establish a society that honours and respects sexual autonomy and fulfilment, regardless of age.

Let's lay down some of these beliefs regarding sexuality as we age in simpler terms:

1. Myth: Sex is only for young people.

Reality: Absolutely not! Sexuality is a lifetime experience, and it's entirely normal and healthy to enjoy sex at any age, including well into your 40s, 50s, 60s, and beyond. Age doesn't determine your capacity to enjoy pleasure or closeness.

2. Myth: Older individuals aren't interested in sex.

Reality: This couldn't be further from the truth. Many elderly folks continue to have active and rewarding sex lives. While wants and tastes may alter with time, it's crucial to remember that sexual attraction doesn't evaporate with age. In fact, some individuals may discover that they grow more daring and open-minded as they become older.

3. Myth: Older bodies aren't capable of enjoying sex.

Reality: Our bodies may alter as we age, but that doesn't imply they're any less capable of enjoying pleasure. With age typically comes knowledge and a greater awareness of what feels good. Plus, there are many methods to adapt and explore new routes of pleasure, whether it's through talking with your partner, trying out alternative techniques, or introducing aids like lubricants or sex toys.

4. Myth: Older folks shouldn't talk about sex.

Reality: Open talk about sex is necessary at any age, particularly later in life. In fact, it might be even more vital as we age, especially when coping with challenges like changes in desire, physical restrictions, or health concerns. Talking freely and honestly with your partner about your wants, desires, and any issues you may be encountering can help build your relationship and increase your sexual encounters.

5. Myth: Sex is exclusively about penetration.

Reality: Sexuality is complex and multifaceted, and it's not confined to penetrative intercourse. There are various ways to enjoy pleasure and closeness, from sensuous touch and kissing to oral sex, mutual masturbation, and more. As we mature, it's crucial to extend our idea of sex and discover what feels good and rewarding for us personally.

6. Myth: Older persons should feel ashamed or embarrassed about their sexuality.

Reality: Absolutely not! Sexuality is a natural and normal element of being human, and there's no need to feel guilty or embarrassed about it, regardless of your age. Everyone deserves to feel comfortable and powerful in their sexual identity, and there's no shame in expressing your desires and needs.

7. Myth: Older folks can't have fulfilling sex lives.

Reality: Satisfaction in sex is subjective and varies from person to person. While it's true that certain physical changes may occur as we age, such as changes in hormone levels or erectile function, these changes don't always indicate that sex can't be pleasant. With open conversation, experimentation, and a willingness to adapt, older individuals may continue to have highly rewarding and joyful sex lives.

8. Myth: Older folks don't require sex education or sexual health care.

Reality: Sexual health is crucial at every age, particularly later in life. Older individuals may confront specific sexual health problems, such as managing chronic health conditions, negotiating changes in libido, or addressing concerns connected to menopause or erectile dysfunction. Access to comprehensive sex education and sexual health care services is vital for enhancing overall well-being and quality of life.

9. Myth: Older folks can't explore their sexuality or attempt new activities.

Reality: Age should never be a barrier to developing your sexuality or trying new activities. In fact, many older folks discover that they have a renewed sense of independence and confidence to explore their goals and preferences. Whether it's trying out new positions, experimenting with different types of stimulation, or exploring fantasies, there's no end to the possibilities for sexual expression at any age.

10. Myth: Older individuals shouldn't value pleasure or closeness.

Reality: Pleasure and closeness are crucial parts of total well-being, regardless of age. Older people need to focus on their sexual pleasure and closeness just as much as anybody else. Whether it's through solitary exploration, personal times with a spouse, or connecting with a new love interest, emphasising pleasure and intimacy may boost happiness, fulfilment, and overall quality of life.

"The Ageless Orgasm" intends to inspire readers to embrace their sexuality, overcome age-related restrictions, and create healthy and gratifying sex lives long into midlife and beyond.

Chapter One:

Understanding Changes in Midlife Sexuality

As we travel through midlife, our bodies and minds go through a series of changes that can significantly impact our sexuality. These changes are influenced by a range of conditions, including biological ageing, hormone swings, emotional alterations, and psychological adaptations. In this chapter, we'll look at these alterations in greater depth to obtain a deeper understanding of how they impact our sexual experiences.

One of the most visible features of midlife sexuality is the physical changes that occur in our bodies. As we age, our hormone levels fluctuate, leading to changes in desire, arousal, and sexual function. For example, males may suffer a reduction in testosterone levels, which can result in diminished libido and erectile problems. Similarly, women may suffer menopause, characterised by reductions in estrogen levels, vaginal dryness, and lower sexual desire.

These bodily changes can have a big influence on our sexual encounters. They may influence our capacity to become aroused, attain orgasm, or continue sexual activity for lengthy durations. Additionally, changes in sexual function can lead to emotions of frustration, shame, or inadequacy, undermining our confidence and self-esteem in the bedroom.

In addition to physical changes, midlife sexuality is also affected by emotional and psychological transformations. As we age, we may face changes in our priorities, relationships, and living circumstances, which can impair our emotional well-being and general happiness with sex.

For example, midlife frequently carries with it greater obligations, such as caring for elderly parents or managing job demands, which can leave us feeling anxious, weary, or overwhelmed. These mental strains might bleed over into our sex life, resulting in diminished desire, closeness, or pleasure.

Moreover, midlife is a period of contemplation and self-discovery, where we may rethink our values, ambitions, and desires. This reflection can lead to alterations in our sexual identity, preferences, and expectations, as we attempt to fit our sexual encounters with our growing sense of ourselves.

Hormonal variations have a key influence in midlife sexuality, particularly for women undergoing menopause and males experiencing andropause. These hormonal shifts can affect several areas of sexual health, including libido, vaginal health, and sexual function.

During menopause, for example, decreased estrogen levels can lead to symptoms such as hot flashes, mood swings, and vaginal dryness, which can impact sexual desire and comfort. Similarly, males may suffer a reduction in testosterone levels, resulting in changes in desire, energy levels, and sexual function.

Managing these hormonal shifts can be tough, but it's crucial to seek assistance and tools to manage symptoms successfully. Hormone replacement therapy, lifestyle adjustments, and alternative therapies can help reduce symptoms and enhance overall sexual health and well-being.

Understanding changes in midlife sexuality entails acknowledging the interaction of physical, emotional, and hormonal elements that impact our sexual experiences. By identifying and addressing these changes, we may traverse midlife sexuality with confidence, resilience, and a dedication to sustaining meaningful and gratifying sex lives.

1. Physical Changes and Their Impact on Sexuality:

Physical changes in midlife could affect how we feel sex. As we age, our bodies go through many changes that might impair our sexual health and function. Here are several significant bodily changes and their implications on sexuality:

1. Hormonal Shifts: Hormones are like messengers in our body that affect things like our sex desire and how our bodies perform sexually. As we get older, these hormone levels might vary, and that can alter how we feel and perform sexually.

For women, a huge shift comes at menopause, which normally occurs around the age of 50. During menopause, the levels of estrogen, a hormone that plays a large role in women's bodies, diminish. This can lead to symptoms including heat flashes, mood swings, and a lack of moisture in the vagina, which can make sex painful or less desirable.

For males, there's a comparable decrease in hormone levels as they age. Testosterone, the hormone that assists with things like sex desire and erections, tends to decline gradually over time. This can lead to a reduction in sex drive and issues achieving or sustaining an erection, which is known as erectile dysfunction.

These variations in hormone levels are natural components of becoming older, but they may obviously alter how we feel and behave sexually. The good news is there are methods to handle these changes and still enjoy a great sex life, whether it's through medication, lifestyle modifications, or conversation with your spouse.

2. Changes in Sensation: As we age, our bodies might not feel as responsive to touch and stimulus as they used to. This might make it tougher to become aroused or to have sexual pleasure. For example, things that used to feel incredibly pleasant might not feel as intense now.

For women, there might be changes in vaginal lubrication, which is the natural moisture that helps make sex pleasant and joyful. As women become older, they may generate less lubrication, which can make intercourse seem dry or even painful.

These changes in feeling are typical components of ageing, but they may obviously impair our sexual experiences. The good news is there are strategies to address these changes and still maintain a satisfying sex life. For example, using lubricants can help make sex more pleasant, and exploring new sorts of touch and stimulation can help keep things exciting and delightful. Communication with your partner is also key—letting them know what feels good and what doesn't will help guarantee that you both have a gratifying and joyful encounter.

3. Chronic Health Conditions: As we become older, we're more likely to develop health conditions that linger around for a long time, such diabetes, high blood pressure, or arthritis. These are called chronic health conditions. They can alter our sexual function and enjoyment in a few distinct ways.

For example, chronic illnesses might cause discomfort, exhaustion, or restrictions in movement, making sex uncomfortable or difficult. Conditions like arthritis could make it hard to move particular portions of our body, which might impact the positions we can try during sex. Diabetes and high blood pressure can also impact blood flow, which is critical for sexual pleasure and function.

Another thing to consider is that the drugs we take to control these problems might have adverse effects that impair our sexual health too. Some drugs could diminish our sex desire, make it difficult to get aroused, or alter our capacity to have an orgasm.

Dealing with chronic health concerns can surely offer obstacles in our sex lives, but there are ways to work around them and still enjoy gratifying sexual encounters. Talking to your doctor about any concerns you have and finding new strategies to manage your illness might help. And remember, communication with your partner is key—being open and honest about how you're feeling and what you need will help guarantee that you both have a satisfying and pleasant sex life.

4. Physical Appearance: As we grow older, our bodies go through natural changes, and these changes might impact how we view ourselves and feel about our sexuality. Things like gaining

weight, getting wrinkles, or seeing changes in muscle tone might alter our body image and how confident we feel about our look.

For example, if we're not content with how our bodies appear, it might make us feel less confident in the bedroom and reduce our desire for sex. We could worry about how our spouse perceives us or feel self-conscious about specific portions of our physique.

These concerns about physical appearance can impair our sexual confidence and desire, making it harder to feel comfortable and enjoy intimacy with our partner. However, it's vital to realise that ageing is a natural process, and everyone's body changes with time.

Finding methods to enjoy and care for our bodies, regardless of how they look, may help enhance our body image and raise our confidence in the bedroom. This could mean practising self-care, engaging in activities that make us feel good about ourselves, or concentrating on the aspects we love about our bodies rather than obsessing on perceived defects.

Ultimately, feeling comfortable and secure in our own skin is crucial to maintaining a meaningful and gratifying sex life as we age. By loving our bodies and fostering our self-esteem, we may build a positive body image that enriches our sexual experiences and increases our relationship with our partner.

5. Stamina and Endurance: As we become older, we can realise that we don't have the same physical energy and endurance that we used to. This can impact how long we're able to participate in sexual activity and how energetic we can be.

For example, we could feel more weary or drained, which might make it harder to keep up with longer or more intense sexual activities. This could lead to emotions of dissatisfaction or disappointment, especially if we're used to having greater stamina in the past.

These changes in stamina and endurance are typical components of ageing, and it's vital to know that our bodies might not be able to achieve the same things they once could. However, it's also crucial to remember that sex isn't just about how long it lasts or how vigorous it is—it's about the connection and closeness we feel with our partner.

Finding strategies to adapt and adjust to these changes, such as trying alternative positions or taking pauses when needed, can help us continue to enjoy gratifying sexual encounters as we age. Communication with our partner is also key—being open and honest about how we're feeling and what we need may help guarantee that we both have a satisfying and pleasant sex relationship.

2. Emotional and Psychological Shifts

As we age, our feelings and attitudes about sex might change, and this may influence how we feel and behave in the bedroom. Several significant emotional and psychological alterations that might influence our sexuality may include:

1. Changing Priorities: As we age, our focus and what we value in life might change. This can alter how much time and energy we have for sex. Let us have a closer look at how shifting priorities might affect our sexuality:

1. Career, Family, and Health: As we grow older, we could become more focused on our professions, taking care of our families, or preserving our health. This shift in emphasis might mean that we have less time and energy to dedicate to sex. We can find ourselves balancing job duties, taking care of children or elderly parents, or coping with health difficulties, leaving us with less time and energy for intimacy.

2. Relationship requirements: As we mature, we can start to think more about what we want from our relationships and if our sexual encounters are serving our requirements. We could emphasise emotional connection, closeness, or friendship over physical pleasure. This can lead to a shift in how we approach sex, concentrating more on quality rather than quantity and seeking deeper relationships with our partners.

3. Contemplation and Evaluation: With age comes knowledge and contemplation. We could start to review our prior experiences and relationships, analysing what has worked well for us and what hasn't. This contemplation can lead to a higher knowledge of our wants and desires, altering how we approach sex and relationships in the future. We could become more picky about who we choose to be intimate with and prioritise

relationships that please us emotionally and sexually.

2. Relationship Dynamics: As we grow older, our relationships with our partners might change, and this can affect our sexuality. How these changes in relationship dynamics might affect our sex lives include:

1. Closeness and Connection: As we negotiate life together, we could get closer to our companion. Sharing experiences, experiencing problems, and maturing together may deepen our link and improve our emotional connection. This proximity can boost intimacy and desire, leading to more pleasurable sexual encounters.

2. Distance and Disconnection: On the other side, we can find ourselves feeling more distant or detached from our partner as we age. Life's stressors, such as job, family commitments, or health worries, can take a toll on our relationship and create hurdles to intimacy. This distance can lead to a decline in desire for sex and a feeling of separation in the bedroom.

3. Communication and Understanding: Effective communication is crucial to sustaining a healthy

and rewarding relationship. As we mature, we could grow better at talking with our spouse, expressing our wants, wishes, and worries more honestly. This can build understanding and empathy, increasing our relationship and enriching our sexual experiences.

4. Changes in Sexual tastes: Our sexual tastes and wants might develop over time, and this can affect our relationship dynamics. We could discover new interests or wants as we mature, leading to changes in how we express ourselves sexually with our spouse. Open conversation and reciprocal inquiry may help us negotiate these changes and keep our partnership vibrant and intriguing.

3. Self-Image and Confidence: As we get older, how we view ourselves and how confident we feel might change, and this can impact our sexuality. Let us look closely at how changes in self-image and confidence might affect our sex lives:

1. Worries About Appearance and Performance: As we age, we could become more anxious about how we appear or how well we perform in bed. We could worry about things like wrinkles, weight gain, or not being as physically fit as we once

were. These anxieties can damage our confidence and make us feel less comfortable in our own skin, which can impair our desire for sex and our enjoyment with our sexual encounters.

2. Comfort and Acceptance: On the other side, we could feel more comfortable and accepting of ourselves as we age. We could accept our faults and cherish our bodies for what they are. This attitude of self-acceptance may enhance our confidence and make us feel more confident in our sexuality, leading to greater enjoyment with our sexual encounters.

3. Communication and Connection: Feeling confident in ourselves may also boost our capacity to speak with our spouse and connect emotionally. When we feel good about ourselves, we're more willing to communicate our wants, desires, and worries freely and honestly. This can deepen our connection and increase our sexual experiences, leading to deeper closeness and happiness.

4. Exploring and Experimenting: Confidence in ourselves can also encourage us to explore and experiment sexually. We could feel more eager to try new things, communicate our wishes, and take risks in the bedroom. This spirit of

exploration may make our sex lives fresh and gratifying, even as we age.

4. Emotional Well-being:
Our emotional well-being has a huge impact on how we feel about sex, and it can alter as we age. Here's a closer look at how changes in mental health might affect our sex lives:

1. Stress, Anxiety, and Depression: Feeling pressured, nervous, or sad can make it harder to enjoy sex. These unpleasant feelings might impair our mood, energy levels, and interest in sex. For example, stress from work or family commitments could distract us during intimate times, while anxiety or sadness might make us feel less driven or interested in being intimate with our spouse.

2. Happiness and Relaxation: On the other hand, feeling joyful, calm, and connected to our partner might increase our sexual experiences. When we're in a great mood and feeling emotionally fulfilled, we're more likely to be aroused and enjoy sex. For example, spending quality time with our partner, engaging in activities we like, or practising relaxation techniques like deep breathing or meditation can help relieve stress

and enhance a sense of well-being, making sex more pleasant.

3. Communication and Support: Open communication and support from our spouse may also significantly affect our mental well-being and our sex life. Being able to discuss frankly about our feelings, wants, and desires may enhance our link and build a sense of trust and closeness. Feeling supported and understood by our partner may help ease tension and anxiety, making it easier to relax and enjoy sex.

4. Seeking Help: If we're battling with negative feelings that are harming our sex life, it's crucial to seek help from a healthcare practitioner or therapist. They may give support, guidance, and resources to help enhance our mental well-being and address any underlying issues that may be harming our sex life. This could entail therapy, medication, or lifestyle modifications to assist manage stress, anxiety, or depression.

5. Cultural and Societal Influences: Our views and attitudes regarding sex are impacted by the culture and society we're part of, and they might change as we mature. How cultural and societal influences might affect our sexuality:

1. Open-mindedness and Acceptance: As we grow older, we could become more open-minded and accepting of other sexualities and lifestyles. This can involve becoming more supportive of LGBTQ+ rights, campaigning for sexual freedom, and questioning established gender roles. We might accept variety and appreciate the uniqueness of each individual's sexual identity and preferences.

2. Conservatism and Tradition: On the other side, as we age, we could also become more conservative and traditional in our ideas regarding sex. We could hang onto conventional ideals and views about marriage, monogamy, and sexual morality. We could be more cautious or critical about sexual activities that stray from society standards or expectations.

3. Impact on Sexual Expression: These cultural and societal factors might alter how we express ourselves sexually and what we think to be normal or acceptable. For example, if we live in a society that emphasises sexual modesty and restraint, we could feel more reserved or constrained in expressing our desires or exploring our sexuality freely. Conversely, if we live in a society that encourages sexual freedom and exploration, we could feel more empowered

to accept our impulses and express ourselves truthfully.

4. Changing viewpoints: Our attitudes and views regarding sex might develop over time when we're exposed to new ideas, experiences, and viewpoints. We could criticise outmoded or restricted cultural conventions and push for more sexual freedom and equality. Alternatively, we could find comfort and stability in old values and beliefs, attempting to maintain them in a quickly changing environment.

Emotional and psychological adjustments can have a substantial influence on our sexuality as we age. By recognizing and exploring these changes, we may better manage our sexual experiences and relationships and continue to enjoy meaningful and gratifying sex lives well into midlife and beyond.

3. Navigating Hormonal Changes

Hormonal changes are normal processes that occur in our bodies as we age. These changes can influence several elements of our health and well-being, including our sexuality. Here's a closer look at handling hormonal changes:

1. Understanding Hormones: Hormones are like little messengers in our bodies that inform different areas of our body what to do. They play a huge influence in things like our sex drive and how our reproductive system operates. As we become older, the amounts of these hormones might alter, and this can cause changes in our bodies and how we feel.

For example, women go through a phase called menopause as they become older. During menopause, the levels of estrogen, one of the major hormones in women's bodies, fall. This can lead to symptoms including heat flashes, mood swings, and changes in the vagina that can make sex painful.

Men also undergo changes in hormones as they age. Testosterone, a hormone that's vital for things like sex desire and physical strength, tends to decline gradually over time. This can lead to things like a reduction in sex drive, trouble attaining or sustaining an erection, and changes in mood.

These variations in hormone levels are natural components of becoming older, but they may obviously alter how we feel and behave sexually. The good news is there are methods to manage these changes and still enjoy a great sex life, whether it's through medication, lifestyle modifications, or talking to a healthcare specialist.

2. Menopause and Andropause: Menopause and andropause are normal processes that occur as individuals become older.

1. Menopause: This is something that happens to women, generally around the age of 50. During menopause, a woman's body generates less estrogen, which is a hormone that assists with things like menstruation and keeping the vagina moist. As estrogen levels decline, women could suffer symptoms including hot flashes, mood swings, and dryness in the vagina, which can make intercourse painful.

2. Andropause: This is frequently dubbed "male menopause," because it happens to males, generally starting in their 40s or 50s. During andropause, a man's body generates less testosterone, which is a hormone that assists with things like sex desire and physical strength. As testosterone levels fall, men could experience symptoms including a diminished sex desire, feeling more exhausted, and having problems attaining or holding an erection.

Both menopause and andropause are natural processes of ageing, although they can produce changes in the body and how people feel. The good news is there are methods to control symptoms and still enjoy a great sex life, whether it's through medication, lifestyle modifications, or talking to a healthcare specialist.

3. Impact on Sexuality: Hormonal shifts might alter our sexual health and experiences in major ways.

1. For Women: When estrogen levels decline, it can lead to vaginal dryness, which means the vagina isn't as moist as it used to be. This can make sex unpleasant or even painful. Additionally, decreasing estrogen levels can also induce a drop in libido, which means a woman might not feel as interested in having sex as she used to.

2. For Men: When testosterone levels fall, it might result in a diminished sex drive, meaning a guy might not feel as interested in sex as he used to. Lower testosterone levels can also cause issues establishing or sustaining erections, which means a guy can have trouble acquiring or

holding an erection during sex. This can impact sexual function and enjoyment.

These variations in hormone levels are typical components of ageing, but they can impair sexual health and experiences. The good news is there are methods to control symptoms and still enjoy a great sex life, whether it's through medication, lifestyle modifications, or talking to a healthcare specialist.

4. Managing Symptoms: There are numerous strategies to aid with symptoms produced by hormonal fluctuations and maintain our sexual health in check.

1. For Women: If a woman is going through menopause and experiencing symptoms like hot flashes or vaginal dryness, she could seek hormone replacement treatment (HRT). This entails taking drugs that replace the estrogen that the body is no longer making enough of. These drugs can help reduce discomfort and make sex more comfortable. Additionally, there are additional drugs and lubricants available to aid with vaginal dryness.

2. For Men: If a guy has low testosterone levels and is experiencing symptoms like a diminished sex desire or trouble with erections, he could seek testosterone replacement treatment (TRT). This entails obtaining testosterone through injections, patches, gels, or tablets to assist enhance testosterone levels and improve libido and sexual performance. It's vital to talk to a healthcare physician about the dangers and advantages of TRT before commencing therapy.

3. Lifestyle adjustments: Making specific lifestyle adjustments can help improve hormone balance and general sexual health. Regular exercise, such as walking, swimming, or yoga, can assist improve blood flow and enhance energy levels, which can benefit sexual function. Eating a balanced diet rich in fruits, vegetables, whole grains, and lean meats can help improve general health and hormone balance. Additionally, exercising stress management strategies like deep breathing, meditation, or mindfulness can help lower stress levels, which can have a favourable influence on sexual health.

By exploring these choices and talking to a healthcare physician, persons suffering symptoms of hormonal shifts can discover strategies to control their symptoms and keep a pleasant sex life.

5. Communication and Support:

1. Open Communication: It's crucial to discuss freely with your spouse about any changes you're feeling due to hormone fluctuations. This involves addressing changes in libido, sexual function, and any discomfort or concerns you may have. Being honest and upfront with your spouse may help enhance your connection and develop understanding and support.

2. Seeking Professional Help: If you're experiencing substantial changes in libido or sexual function, it's crucial to talk to a healthcare specialist. They can assist uncover any underlying concerns and discuss therapy alternatives that may help lessen symptoms. Whether it's hormone replacement treatment, medication, or lifestyle modifications, a healthcare practitioner can give guidance and support targeted to your unique requirements.

3. Maintaining Emotional closeness: Hormonal shifts can affect more than just physical health—they can also impair emotional well-being and closeness in relationships. It's

crucial to preserve emotional closeness and connection with your spouse, even while you negotiate these changes. This involves spending quality time together, showing affection, and supporting each other through both the highs and lows.

4. Navigating Together: Navigating hormonal shifts can be tough, but it's crucial to realise that you're not alone. Lean on your spouse for support and work together as a team to handle any challenges that emerge. By tackling these changes together and maintaining open communication and support, you may negotiate hormonal fluctuations and maintain a joyful and rewarding sex life.

Chapter Two:

Intimate Communication: The Language of Desire

Imagine a world where every word uttered and every action shared between couples is like a secret code unlocking deeper connections and kindling passions. Welcome to "Intimate Communication: This chapter will take you on a journey to explore how communication may alter your relationship.

We are going to dig into the power of honest discourse. We'll discover how communicating your ideas, feelings, and wants with your spouse may improve your relationship and bring you closer together. We'll also address the value of having a judgement-free zone where you and your partner may openly express your thoughts and wants, opening up new pathways of exploration and enjoyment.

But it's not only about words; it's also about actions. We'll explore how tiny gestures of kindness and understanding may build emotional connection, establishing the groundwork for a more meaningful and passionate relationship.

This chapter will present practical advice and tactics for connecting intimately with your spouse, developing a deeper connection, and boosting your sexual relationship. By participating in honest discussion, expressing dreams without judgement, and fostering emotional closeness, you may establish a meaningful and rewarding connection founded on trust, respect, and mutual desire.

In "Ageless Orgasm," personal communication is like the specific language couples use to comprehend one other's wishes and feelings. Here's how it works:

1. Understanding Desires: Couples discuss frankly about what they want and like in the bedroom. This helps them understand one other better and make sex more delightful.

2. Building Emotional Closeness: By discussing their thoughts and feelings, partners get closer emotionally. This connection makes their relationship stronger and their sex life more pleasant.

3. Keeping Passion Alive: Couples communicate about their desires and dreams, which keeps

their passion for each other alive. It's like putting gasoline to the flames of desire.

4. Dealing with Challenges: Sometimes, factors like health concerns or stress might impact sex. But by communicating honestly, couples may discover answers together and overcome these obstacles.

5. Making Sex Better: By speaking during sex, couples can make sure they both feel good and have a fantastic time together. It's all about understanding each other's wants and making sex satisfying for both partners.

Intimate communication is the cornerstone to a good and successful sex life, no matter your age.

1. Deepening Connection via Honest Communication

Communication is like the glue that ties relationships together, especially when it comes to being close with your spouse. Here's why being open and honest with each other about your ideas, feelings, and aspirations is so important:

1. Building Trust: When you're honest with your spouse, it's like opening up a window into your heart and allowing them to see the real you. You're revealing your innermost thoughts and feelings, even if they're not always easy to talk about. This honesty demonstrates that you trust your spouse profoundly. It's like saying, "I believe in you enough to be vulnerable with you."

As you disclose your actual self, your partner learns more about who you are, what matters to you, and how you perceive the world. This improves your relationship since it's like you're creating a bridge of understanding between you two. Your spouse knows they can rely on you to be honest and straightforward, which makes them feel cherished and appreciated.

This honesty also establishes a strong foundation of trust in your partnership. Trust is like the glue that ties everything together. When you trust your spouse and they trust you, it's simpler to rely on one other, support each other, and feel safe in your relationship. You know that you can count on your spouse to be there for you, no matter what.

Being honest with your relationship is like watering a plant. It helps your relationship develop and thrive. So, don't be frightened to communicate your opinions and feelings honestly. It's one of the finest methods to develop a strong, healthy, and happy relationship.

2. Understanding Each Other: When you converse honestly with your relationship, it's like unlocking a treasure trove full of surprises. You both get to discuss what you enjoy, what you don't like, and even those tiny oddities that make you distinct. It's like saying, "Let's get to know each other better!"

As you discuss these things, you learn more about one another's worlds. You discover what makes your spouse smile, what makes them tick, and what makes them feel unique. It's like fitting together pieces of a puzzle to get the broader picture of who they are.

This better understanding draws you closer together, like two jigsaw pieces fitting perfectly. You start to feel more connected because you see each other for who you actually are. It's like saying, "I get you, and I appreciate you just the way you are."
Talking freely helps you understand each other better. It's like uncovering fresh riches in a

treasure hunt. So, keep sharing and listening, since every talk pulls you closer and makes your relationship stronger.

3. Resolving Conflict: When you and your spouse have a dispute or fight, it's like experiencing a bump on the road on your trip together. But if you communicate freely and honestly about what's upsetting you, it's like utilising a map to find your way back on track.

By talking things out quietly and listening to each other, you may find out what went wrong and how to correct it. It's like saying, "Let's work together to solve this problem."

When you handle concerns straight immediately, it's like stopping a minor leak before it escalates into a major flood. It avoids misunderstandings from growing worse and producing upset sentiments. Instead, you may develop answers together and go ahead as a team.

Talking openly about difficulties helps you address them before they become bigger concerns. It's like putting out a fire before it spreads. So, remember to speak with each other, even when things are rough, because working together is the greatest approach to address problems and keep your relationship healthy.

4. Expressing wants: Your spouse isn't a mind reader, therefore it's necessary to discuss your wants and wishes honestly. Whether it's about sex, emotional support, or quality time together, communicating what you need helps guarantee your relationship remains full and rewarding for both of you.

Imagine you're hungry, but you don't tell anyone. Your lover won't know you're hungry until you say anything. It's like asking them to predict what you need without any hints!

When you tell your partner what you need, it's like handing them a blueprint to your heart. You're saying, "Here's what I need to feel happy and loved." This transparency helps them understand you better and makes them more likely to accommodate your requirements.

Whether it's cuddling, help around the home, or simply some alone time, communicating your wants maintains your relationship strong and healthy. It's like watering a plant to make it grow big and robust. So, don't be shy—speak up and

let your spouse know what you need to feel loved
and fulfilled.

5. Creating Intimacy: Intimacy is like having a
best friend who knows everything about you and
still loves you. It's about feeling close and
connected with your lover in a particular manner.

When you share your deepest thoughts and
feelings with your spouse, it's like opening up a
treasure box and exposing them your most
valuable secrets. You're saying, "This is who I
am, and I trust you enough to share it with you."

This transparency establishes a powerful tie
between you two, like making a knot that can't
be severed. You start to feel like you're a team,
fighting life's ups and downs together.

Intimacy is like having a secret handshake that
only you and your spouse know. It's about
feeling secure and cherished, just the way you
are. So, keep sharing and caring, since that's
what makes your friendship stronger every day.

2. Sharing Fantasies and Desires without Judgment

When you and your partner feel comfortable and welcomed to discuss your thoughts and wants without judgement, it's like having a snug sanctuary where you can be your genuine selves. This safe zone allows you both to speak up about your deepest desires, no matter how wild or strange they may appear.

By discussing your dreams, you're letting your partner into your deepest world, showing them a side of you that you may not expose to anyone else. This amount of vulnerability increases your link and deepens your connection, as you both feel fully seen and understood by each other.

Exploring each other's fantasies may offer a whole new depth to your sex life. It's like beginning on a thrilling trip together, where you both get to explore new delights and sensations. This shared discovery generates excitement, closeness, and mutual fulfilment, bringing you even closer as a pair.

Moreover, when you create a judgement-free zone for discussing desires, you build an attitude of trust and acceptance in your partnership. This trust extends beyond the bedroom, impacting how you communicate, support, and care for each other in all parts of your lives.

Creating a secure area to communicate dreams and aspirations without judgement is like cultivating a rare and beautiful flower. It involves care, trust, and understanding, but the benefits are immense—a deeper connection, heightened intimacy, and a richer sex life that keeps the flames of desire burning hot.

Creating a secure environment devoid of judgement in a relationship is highly essential for various reasons:

1. Encourages Open Communication: When individuals feel comfortable and accepted, they are more willing to communicate their views, feelings, and desires freely. This facilitates honest and truthful conversation, leading to a greater understanding and connection between couples.

2. Builds Trust: In a non-judgmental setting, couples feel confident in being candid with one other. This vulnerability creates trust over time, as individuals feel sure that they may disclose their actual selves without fear of judgement or rejection.

3. Strengthens Emotional Intimacy: Sharing without judgement generates a sense of emotional intimacy and acceptance between couples. Knowing that they can be themselves without reservation improves the emotional tie, generating a higher degree of closeness in the partnership.

4. Fosters Mutual Respect: When partners refrain from expressing judgement on each other's ideas, feelings, and wants, it exhibits respect for each other's individuality and autonomy. This mutual respect provides the cornerstone of a healthy and equal collaboration.

5. Promotes Exploration and Growth: A judgement-free place helps individuals to explore new ideas, desires, and experiences without fear of criticism or humiliation. This encourages personal growth and helps couples to discover similar interests and desires, improving their relationship.

Creating a safe environment free of judgement is vital for building a loving, supportive, and happy relationship where both parties feel appreciated, respected, and understood.

3. Cultivating Emotional Intimacy

Cultivating emotional connection is like caring to a fragile garden—it takes care, attention, and nurturing to grow. Here are some basic strategies to increase emotional closeness with your partner:

1. Quality Time Together: Quality time together means spending unique times with your lover, just the two of you. It's like having a date with your best buddy, where you can speak and laugh without any interruptions.

You may do simple things like having a beautiful meal together, taking a stroll while holding hands, or cuddling up on the sofa with a blanket. The main thing is to focus on each other and enjoy being in each other's presence.

When you share these experiences, it's like filling up a treasure box with cherished memories. These moments build a deep tie between you and your lover, making your relationship even more precious. So, be sure to set aside time for each other and appreciate these moments—they're what help your relationship grow stronger every day.

2. Expressing Affection: Expressing affection is like expressing to your spouse how much you care about them in tiny ways. It's like giving them a warm embrace or a lovely kiss to make them feel cherished and treasured.

You may also demonstrate devotion by conducting simple acts of kindness, like leaving a note saying "I love you" or making their favourite food. These gestures show your spouse that you're thinking about them and that you want to make them happy.

When you communicate affection, it's like filling up their heart with warmth and happiness. It enhances your link and makes your relationship stronger. So, don't forget to show your lover how much you love them every time you get—it's the simple things that mean most.

3. Open Communication: Open communication is like having a heart-to-heart chat with your lover, where you express everything without holding back. It's like having a safe area where you can be yourself and share your thoughts and feelings without fear.

To communicate honestly, it's necessary to listen to your spouse without condemning them. This entails actually paying attention to what they're saying and comprehending how they feel. It's like saying, "I hear you, and I understand."

You should also share your own opinions and feelings honestly. Don't be scared to talk about your concerns, dreams, and vulnerabilities with your spouse. It's like opening up a book and letting them read your story—it helps them understand you better and enhances your relationship.

When you talk honestly, it's like creating a bridge between you and your spouse. It establishes a deep connection and makes your bond even stronger. So, be sure to communicate to your spouse honestly and listen to them with an open heart—it's the key to a happy and healthy relationship.

4. Supporting Each Other: Being there for your spouse through both the highs and lows of life fosters emotional connection. This involves expressing support, empathy, and understanding at hard times, as well as recognizing their victories and accomplishments. Knowing that you have each other's backs generates a sense of security and trust in the partnership.

5. Shared Experiences: Sharing new experiences and making memories together enhances emotional connection. Whether it's going to new locations, doing new activities, or following mutual hobbies, shared experiences build a powerful sense of connection and belonging. These shared moments become cherished recollections that enhance the tie between you.

In basic terms, establishing emotional closeness with your spouse is about spending quality time together, displaying love, speaking honestly, supporting each other, and sharing experiences. By fostering these components of your relationship, you may establish a stronger connection and a more rewarding and meaningful partnership.

Chapter Three:

Rediscovering Pleasure

Rediscovering pleasure beyond the age of 40 is an exciting adventure that requires learning new methods to enjoy closeness and connection with our partners. As we age, our bodies change, and so do our aspirations and tastes. But that doesn't mean our sex lives have to diminish — in fact, they may become even more meaningful and pleasurable with the correct mentality and approach.

One method to find pleasure beyond 40 is by discovering new erogenous zones – those specific parts of our bodies that react to touch and stimulation. These zones could alter as we mature, so it's crucial to be interested and open to discovering new sources of pleasure. Taking the time to investigate our bodies and talk with our partners about what feels good may lead to fascinating new experiences in the bedroom.

Experimenting with ways for boosting arousal and feeling is another key component of finding pleasure after 40. This might entail trying new forms of touch, positions, or activities to find what offers us the greatest pleasure. It's all about keeping open-minded and eager to discover new things along with our partners. Fantasy and imagination also play an important role in sexual enjoyment, regardless of age. Embracing our imaginations and sharing them with our partners may bring excitement and spice to our sex life. Whether it's role-playing, reading sexy literature, or viewing sensual movies together, engaging in our imaginations may fuel passion and desire.

Communication is essential along this path of rediscovery. Being upfront and honest with our partners about our desires, fantasies, and boundaries promotes a safe and supportive atmosphere for exploration. By being interested, communicative, and open-minded, individuals and couples may continue to enjoy a full and gratifying sex life well into their 40s and beyond.

Rediscovering pleasure beyond 40 is all about keeping interested, trying new things, and appreciating the importance of fantasy and imagination in our sexual experiences. With communication and transparency, we may continue to experience intimacy and connection with our relationships for years to come.

1. Exploring New Erogenous Zones:

As we age, our bodies change, and so do our erogenous zones—the parts of our bodies that are particularly receptive to sexual stimulation. While certain erogenous zones may remain steady throughout our lives, others may become more receptive or newly found with age. Exploring these additional erogenous zones might bring excitement and freshness to our sexual encounters beyond 40.

1. Sensitivity Shifts: As we get older, our bodies might endure changes in how they sense feelings, especially during intimate situations. Certain regions of our body, such the nipples, neck, ears, and inner thighs, could start to feel more sensitive than previously. This implies that when these regions are touched or aroused, they might cause higher emotions of pleasure and excitement.

Exploring these sensitive regions with your spouse may be a fascinating way to explore new sensations and deepen intimacy. You could notice that light touches or kisses in certain regions feel particularly wonderful. It's all about taking the time to explore and experiment together, enjoying the adventure of learning what offers each other pleasure.

By paying attention to these shifts in sensitivity and discovering new ways to touch and be touched, you and your spouse may strengthen your connection and make your intimate times even more joyful and rewarding.

2. Erotic Mapping: Erotic mapping is like going on an excursion to explore your body or your partner's body to locate the locations that feel particularly wonderful when touched. These particular regions are termed erogenous zones. They're places that are especially sensitive and can make you feel tingling or thrilled when they're touched or stimulated in the proper manner.

When you undertake sexual mapping, you take your time to softly touch different regions of the body to discover how they feel. You could uncover new locations that you weren't aware might deliver pleasure previously. By trying different sorts of touch—like delicate strokes, kisses, or gentle caresses—you may discover what feels the best for you or your partner.

The key to erotic mapping is communication. Talking candidly with your spouse about what feels good and what doesn't helps you both understand each other's bodies better. It's like sharing a secret map of pleasure that only you two know about! This type of exploration may bring you closer together and make your private times even more pleasant and delightful.

3. Mindfulness and Sensation: Mindfulness implies being fully present and focused on what you're feeling in the moment. When you incorporate mindfulness into your sexual practices, it's like paying close attention to the feelings and sensations you're experiencing in your body right then and there.

By being conscious during sex, you may tune in to how different touches and motions make you feel. It's like cranking up the volume on your senses, so you notice every small tingling or shiver of pleasure. This heightened awareness might make the encounter more intense and delightful.

When you're aware during sex, you're not thinking about anything else but what's happening in that moment. This makes you feel more connected to your body and your lover. It's like you're both totally there and focused on one other, which may lead to even more pleasurable and rewarding sexual encounters.

2. Techniques for Enhancing Arousal and Sensation:

As we age, our sexual reactions may alter, needing new approaches and strategies to maximise arousal and experience. Exploring diverse strategies can help individuals and couples maintain a full and satisfied sex life well into their 40s and beyond.

1. Sensate Focus:
Sensate focus is like a specific technique of caressing and exploring each other's bodies to build intimacy and enjoyment without necessarily having sex. It's all about taking turns with your spouse to touch and feel each other in a delicate and generous way.

During sensate focus, you focus on the physical sensations and how your partner's body responds to your touch. It's not about attempting to turn each other on or hurrying to reach a specific point. Instead, it's about enjoying the moment and paying attention to how your partner's body feels beneath your touch.

This approach can make you and your partner feel more connected to each other and more comfortable with your body. It promotes trust and closeness by allowing you to explore and share your bodies in a safe and caring setting. Plus, it can also contribute to heightened sexual desire and excitement when you're ready to take things further.

2. Communication and Feedback:
When it comes to having satisfactory and joyful sex, discussing honestly with your spouse is incredibly crucial. This involves communicating what you enjoy, what you don't like, and what you're comfortable with. It's like making sure you're both on the same page and feeling comfortable about what's occurring.

During sex, it's helpful to let your partner know what feels nice and what doesn't. This might be as easy as stating, "I love it when you touch me like that" or "Could you try something a bit gentler?" Giving feedback helps your spouse understand what you appreciate and how they might make things even better.

Having open communication and offering feedback fosters a secure and supportive atmosphere where both partners may express their wishes and preferences. It's like working together as a team to make sure everyone's having a fantastic time. Plus, when you know what your spouse enjoys, it may lead to even greater pleasure and excitement for both of you.

3. Variety and Experimentation:
Imagine sex as a vast adventure playground where you and your partner may try out all sorts of fascinating things! Variety and experimentation entail changing things up and trying new items to keep things fresh and exciting.

This might be anything from trying out different postures or approaches to exploring new sensations and activities together. It's like adding some spice to your sex life by being open to new experiences and thoughts.

When you're open to exploring new things, you could discover new methods to feel pleasure and excitement that you never knew existed. It's all about having an open mind and being ready to move out of your comfort zone a little bit. Plus, it may make your sex life feel fresh and exciting, like a new experience waiting to be explored!

3. The Role of Fantasy and Imagination in Sexual Fulfilment

Fantasy and imagination have a major part in sexual arousal and pleasure, regardless of age. Exploring fantasies and adding imagination into sexual interactions may kindle passion, inspire desire, and deepen closeness between lovers.

1. Erotic Fantasies:
Erotic fantasies are like movies we play in our thoughts, except they're all about sensual stuff. It's when we picture alternative scenarios or events that turn us on and make us feel thrilled.

When we imagine, we might let our imaginations go wild. We could visualise ourselves in romantic circumstances, trying out new things in the bedroom, or even having adventures with someone special. These dreams may be anything we want them to be, and they're a chance for us to explore our deepest needs and imaginations in a safe and private area.

Fantasising may also be a technique for us to fulfil wants or desires that we haven't experienced in real life. Maybe we fantasise of getting swept off our feet by a loving companion or attempting something new and daring in bed.

It's like giving ourselves permission to explore our sexuality and experience the pleasure of our dreams.

When we discuss our dreams with our spouse, it's like opening up a window into our deepest desires. It might bring us closer together and generate a sense of closeness since we're being open and honest about what drives us on. Plus, it might offer an exciting new element to our sex lives, creating new ideas and desires to explore together.

2. Role-Playing and Pretend Play:
Role-playing is like playing make-believe but for grown-ups. It's when you and your partner pretend to be various personalities or act out amusing scenarios to make sex more pleasurable.

When you role-play, you could dress up in costumes or pretend to be someone else, like a seductive nurse or a brave spy. You may let your imagination go wild and invent all sorts of interesting and daring situations to explore together.

Role-playing is a way for couples to liven things up and explore new things in the bedroom. It's like adding a touch of drama and excitement to your sex life, making it feel like you're starring in your very own sexy movie.

By pretending to be someone else or acting out dreams, role-playing may make you and your spouse feel more adventurous and open-minded. Plus, it may be a wonderful method to engage and connect with each other on a deeper level.

3. Erotic Literature and Media:
Erotic literature and media are like novels or movies that are all about sensual stuff. It's when you read sexy novels, see spicy flicks, or listen to dirty audio that gets you feeling stimulated.

When you immerse yourself in sexual literature or media, it's like walking into a realm of imagination and desire. You may explore all types of dreams, urges, and fetishes in a safe and private way, without any judgement.

These books, videos, or audio snippets might give you ideas for attempting new activities in the bedroom and help you discover more about what turns you on. It's like having a hidden toolbox full of interesting and exciting methods to spice up your sex life.

Exploring sensual books and media may also be a way to bond with your spouse and share your desires together. You may read a sensual book together or watch a romantic movie, creating new ideas and wanting to explore together. Plus, it's a fun and delightful way to add some excitement to your sex life!

Communication is vital as we traverse the road of finding pleasure and intimacy. When we're upfront and honest with our partners about our desires, fantasies, and boundaries, it offers a safe and supportive environment for exploration.

By communicating our ideas and feelings freely, we may create trust and improve our relationship with our spouse. This helps us to explore new experiences and dreams together, knowing that we're both on the same page and respecting each other's boundaries.

Staying inquisitive implies being willing to try new things and explore different facets of our sexuality. It's about being open to new ideas and experiences, and not being hesitant to articulate our wants and desires.

Being communicative implies expressing oneself clearly and listening to our partner's goals and needs. It's about having open and honest talks, even if they can seem a bit awkward at first. This helps guarantee that both parties feel heard and understood, and may freely express themselves without judgement.

And lastly, keeping open-minded requires being willing to learn and develop together. It's about embracing change and being adaptive as we continue to explore our sexuality and relationship.

By embracing these concepts of communication, curiosity, and open-mindedness, individuals and couples may create a long and joyful sex life well into their 40s and beyond. It's all about creating a caring and loving environment where both partners feel free to express themselves and explore their desires together.

Chapter Four:

Overcoming Challenges

As we go through the process of regaining pleasure and intimacy in our 40s and beyond, it's crucial to know that problems may occur along the path. These issues can emerge in numerous forms, from bodily changes like erectile dysfunction and menopause to mental struggles such as stress and weariness. However, by understanding these difficulties and using appropriate tactics, we may sail past them and continue to enjoy a meaningful and gratifying sex life.

Overcoming these problems in our sexual journey involves a combination of recognition, proactive measures, and seeking appropriate help when required. By addressing common issues such as erectile dysfunction and menopause, implementing stress management techniques, and seeking professional help when necessary, individuals and couples can navigate through obstacles and continue to enjoy a fulfilling and satisfying sex life well into their 40s and beyond.

1. Addressing Common Issues:

One typical difficulty that many persons confront as they age is erectile dysfunction (ED) and menopause. ED can affect males of all ages, but it gets more widespread as we get older. It can be caused by several circumstances, including underlying health issues, drug side effects, or psychological factors. Similarly, menopause represents a dramatic hormonal transition in women's bodies, leading to symptoms including hot flashes, vaginal dryness, and changes in libido. By confronting these common concerns head-on and getting proper medical counsel and treatment, individuals may overcome these impediments and restore their sexual vigour.

1. Erectile Dysfunction (ED):
Erectile dysfunction is a widespread worry among men, particularly as they age. It happens when a man struggles to acquire or maintain an erection robust enough for sexual activity. It is a frequent condition defined by the inability to obtain or maintain an erection sufficient for sexual intercourse. It's crucial to understand the numerous variables that might contribute to this disease, since it frequently involves a combination of medical, psychological, and lifestyle problems. Various causes can contribute to ED, including:

1. Underlying Health Disorders: Underlying health disorders can play a significant impact in the development of erectile dysfunction. Conditions such as diabetes, heart disease, high blood pressure (hypertension), and obesity can impede blood flow to the penis or damage neurons and tissues involved in the erection process. For example, diabetes can damage blood vessels and nerves, making it difficult for adequate blood to flow into the penis during arousal, resulting in erectile issues.

2. Medication Adverse Effects: Certain drugs used to treat various health concerns might have adverse effects that interfere with erectile performance. drugs such as beta-blockers (used to treat high blood pressure), antidepressants, antipsychotics, and drugs for prostate disorders can all contribute to erectile dysfunction. These drugs may influence blood flow, hormone levels, or neurotransmitter function, making it hard to get or sustain an erection.

3. Psychological Issues: Psychological issues might also play a key role in erectile dysfunction. Stress, worry, depression, and relationship issues can all contribute to performance anxiety and limit sexual desire. Negative thoughts and feelings around sexual activity can create a cycle

of worry and avoidance, further intensifying the condition. Additionally, prior traumatic events or disagreements within the partnership might influence sexual function and closeness.

Addressing erectile dysfunction (ED) involves a comprehensive strategy that addresses both medical and lifestyle issues. Here are some ways typically used to manage ED:

1. Medical Assessment: It's vital to meet with a healthcare expert to undergo a full medical assessment. This may entail checking for underlying health concerns such as diabetes, heart disease, or hormone imbalances that might be contributing to ED. Identifying and addressing these underlying disorders is critical for enhancing erectile function.

2. Drugs: Prescription drugs known as phosphodiesterase type 5 (PDE5) inhibitors, such as Viagra (sildenafil), Cialis (tadalafil), and Levitra (vardenafil), are routinely administered to assist enhance blood flow to the penis and aid erections. These drugs operate by enhancing the effects of nitric oxide, a substance that relaxes muscles in the penis, allowing for greater blood flow.

3. Lifestyle Adjustments: Making healthy lifestyle adjustments can also assist enhance erectile function. This involves engaging in regular physical exercise, keeping a healthy weight, following a balanced diet rich in fruits, vegetables, whole grains, and lean meats, limiting alcohol use, and quitting smoking. These lifestyle alterations can enhance overall cardiovascular health, which is critical for erectile function.

4. Therapy: Counselling or therapy may be effective for treating any psychological reasons leading to ED, such as stress, anxiety, depression, or relationship troubles. Therapy can help individuals build coping mechanisms, increase communication with their partner, and address any unpleasant thoughts or feelings around sexual activity.

5. Alternative Therapies: Some persons may seek alternative therapies or supplements for ED, such as herbal medicines, acupuncture, or pelvic floor exercises (Kegels). While these procedures may give some assistance for select individuals, it's crucial to contact a healthcare expert before trying any alternative therapies to ensure safety and efficacy.

Resolving erectile dysfunction frequently involves a combination of therapies suited to the individual's personal requirements and circumstances. By working closely with a healthcare physician and implementing positive lifestyle adjustments, many persons may effectively treat ED and enhance their sexual health and quality of life.

2. Menopause:
Menopause is a normal process that happens to women as they become older, generally in their late 40s or early 50s. During menopause, the body goes through major changes, mostly due to a drop in estrogen, a hormone that plays a big part in the menstrual cycle and reproductive system. Here are some common symptoms of menopause:

1. Hot Flashes: These abrupt bursts of heat can vary in severity and frequency, affecting everyday activities and sleep habits. They're triggered by changes in the hypothalamus, the portion of the brain that regulates body temperature. Managing hot flashes may entail wearing lightweight clothing, avoiding spicy foods, staying hydrated, and practising relaxation techniques like deep breathing or meditation.

2. Vaginal Dryness: Declining estrogen levels contribute to weakening and drying of the vaginal tissues, resulting in discomfort or pain during sexual intercourse, itching, or irritation. Using water-based lubricants or vaginal moisturisers can help reduce dryness and increase sexual comfort. Hormone replacement treatment (HRT), estrogen creams, or vaginal rings may also be administered to restore vaginal moisture and suppleness.

3. Changes in Libido: Fluctuations in sexual desire and arousal are frequent throughout menopause, impacting each woman differently. While some may experience a drop in libido owing to hormonal changes, others may see an increase in sexual desire. Emotional variables, such as stress, sadness, or relationship troubles, can also impact libido. Open conversation with a partner, exploring new sexual activities or fantasies, and getting support from a healthcare practitioner or therapist can help handle fluctuations in libido and sustain closeness.

Additionally, menopause can bring along additional symptoms such as mood fluctuations, sleep difficulties, weight gain, and changes in hair and skin. Lifestyle adjustments including regular exercise, a balanced diet rich in calcium and vitamin D, proper sleep, and stress management strategies can help ease these symptoms and enhance general well-being throughout menopause.

It's necessary for women undergoing menopause to have frequent check-ups with their healthcare practitioner to evaluate symptoms, discuss treatment choices, and address any concerns or questions they may have. Every woman's experience with menopause is unique, so tailored treatment and support are vital for navigating this transitional era of life.

Addressing menopausal symptoms involves:

1. Hormone Replacement Therapy (HRT): HRT involves taking drugs that contain female hormones (estrogen and occasionally progesterone) to replace the hormones the body no longer makes after menopause. It can help reduce symptoms including hot flashes, vaginal dryness, and mood changes. However, HRT isn't good for everyone and may have dangers, such as an increased risk of some malignancies or blood clots. It's vital to consider the possible advantages and hazards of HRT with a healthcare practitioner to make an educated decision.

- HRT comes in different forms, including tablets, patches, lotions, and vaginal rings. The kind and dose of hormones administered vary on individual requirements and health factors.

- Estrogen treatment can successfully reduce symptoms including hot flashes, night sweats, and vaginal dryness by replacing hormone levels in the body.

- Some women may also benefit from combination estrogen and progesterone treatment, especially if they have an intact uterus, to minimise the risk of endometrial cancer.

- However, HRT is not without hazards. Long-term usage may raise the risk of breast cancer, stroke, blood clots, and cardiovascular problems. It's crucial to assess the possible advantages against the hazards and share any concerns with a healthcare practitioner.

- For women who are not candidates for or choose not to utilise HRT, other medications such as selective estrogen receptor modulators (SERMs), antidepressants, or gabapentin may give relief from menopausal symptoms.

2. Vaginal Lubricants and Moisturisers:
Over-the-counter vaginal lubricants and moisturisers can give brief relief from vaginal dryness and discomfort during sexual activity. Water-based lubricants are advised as they're less prone to produce irritation or allergic responses. Applying a vaginal moisturiser consistently can also help restore moisture and suppleness to the vaginal tissues over time.

- Vaginal lubricants are generally water-based, silicone-based, or oil-based compounds that minimise friction and pain during sexual activity. Water-based lubricants are safe to use with condoms and sex toys and are simply rinsed off with water.

- Vaginal moisturisers, on the other hand, are meant to hydrate and restore moisture to the vaginal tissues over time. They are administered routinely, generally every few days, to preserve vaginal health and comfort.

- Both lubricants and moisturisers are available over the counter and can be used as required to reduce vaginal dryness and pain. It's crucial to pick goods that are free of irritants and allergies and suitable with particular preferences and sensitivities.1

3. Discussion: Open and honest discussion with a partner regarding menopausal symptoms and their influence on sexual intimacy is crucial. Discussing concerns, desires, and strategies to alter sexual activity to meet changes can develop understanding and support between couples. It's crucial to approach these talks with empathy, patience, and a willingness to listen and compromise.

- Effective communication is the cornerstone of a successful and enjoyable sexual relationship, especially during periods of transition like menopause.

- Couples should provide a secure and supportive atmosphere for open communication regarding menopausal symptoms, sexual urges, and preferences. This may entail setting aside specific time for conversations, actively listening to each other's issues, and demonstrating empathy and understanding.

- Partners can work together to explore alternative sexual activities, experiment with new approaches, and adjust to changes in sexual function and arousal. Mutual understanding and collaboration can increase closeness and connection in the relationship.

4. Exploration of Other Sexual Activities:
Exploring other sexual activities that focus on pleasure and closeness, rather than penetrative intercourse, might be useful during menopause. Sensual massage, mutual masturbation, oral sex, and utilising sex toys can give delightful and rewarding encounters without the pressure of performance or concerns about vaginal dryness. Experimenting with new approaches and activities can help preserve sexual happiness and connection between partners.

- Menopause gives a chance for individuals and couples to widen their sexual repertoire and explore different types of closeness and pleasure.

- Sensuous massage, for example, may be a calming and sensuous method to connect with a partner and stimulate erogenous zones without the pressure of penetrative sex.

- Mutual masturbation allows lovers to discover each other's bodies and pleasure regions, creating connection and mutual happiness.

- Incorporating sex toys, such as vibrators or dildos, into sexual play may boost arousal and pleasure and bring new feelings and experiences.

- Experimenting with different positions, settings, and scenarios can keep sexual activity exciting and fulfilling, even as physical and hormonal changes occur.

By combining these tactics and approaches, individuals and couples may manage the obstacles of menopause with resilience, inventiveness, and intimacy, ensuring that their sexual connection stays full and pleasurable for years to come.

Resolving common sexual difficulties such as erectile dysfunction and menopause needs a comprehensive strategy that addresses physical, psychological, and relationship elements. By getting proper medical counsel and treatment, adopting good lifestyle choices, and encouraging open communication with partners, individuals may overcome these obstacles and recover their sexual vigour in midlife and beyond.

2. Strategies for Managing Stress and Fatigue:

Stress and exhaustion are frequent factors that can severely affect our sex lives, especially when we balance hectic schedules and commitments in midlife. Chronic stress can lead to increased tension in the body, diminished libido, and trouble in obtaining arousal. Fatigue can also lower our energy levels and leave us feeling too exhausted for intimacy. However, by using effective stress management practices such as mindfulness, relaxation exercises, and prioritising self-care, individuals may lower stress levels and enhance their overall well-being. Additionally, providing appropriate rest and sleep can assist overcome exhaustion and raise energy levels, making it simpler to participate in intimate activities.

Strategies for handling stress and exhaustion in greater detail:

A. Mindfulness and Relaxation Techniques:

1. Mindfulness Practices: Mindfulness is the practice of being completely present and engaged in the current moment, without judgement or attachment to ideas or sensations.

Benefits: Mindfulness practices, such as meditation, deep breathing, or body scan exercises, have been demonstrated to relieve stress, anxiety, and depression. By paying attention to the present moment, individuals can create increased awareness, acceptance, and resilience.

Applications: Mindfulness may be practised in numerous locations and activities, including formal meditation sessions, casual mindfulness practices throughout the day, or mindfulness-based therapies such as mindfulness-based stress reduction (MBSR) programs.

Effectiveness: Research shows that regular mindfulness practice can lead to benefits in mental health, emotional well-being, and general quality of life. It can also boost cognitive function, attentional control, and emotional regulation skills.

2. Deep Breathing Exercises: Deep breathing exercises comprise purposeful, slow-paced breathing patterns that engage the body's parasympathetic nervous system, encouraging relaxation and stress reduction.

Common deep breathing techniques include diaphragmatic breathing, box breathing, and 4-7-8 breathing. These techniques focus on prolonging the duration of the exhale and inhale phases, allowing for deeper relaxation and improved oxygenation of the body.

Deep breathing techniques can help ease feelings of stress, worry, and panic by lowering heart rate, reducing muscular tension, and soothing the mind. Regular practice can improve respiratory function, expand lung capacity, and promote overall respiratory health.

3. Meditation Practices: There are different styles of meditation, including mindfulness meditation, loving-kindness meditation, and transcendental meditation. Each method offers distinct ways for increasing present-moment awareness, compassion, and inner serenity.

Beginners may find it beneficial to start with guided meditation sessions, which give guidance and assistance for practising mindfulness or relaxation methods. Guided meditations are available in audio or video forms and cover a wide range of subjects and themes.

Research suggests that regular meditation practice can lead to considerable benefits in mental and emotional well-being, including reduced stress, anxiety, and depression symptoms. Meditation can also boost attention, focus, and emotional resilience over time.

4. Progressive Muscle Relaxation (PMR): Progressive muscle relaxation includes systematically tensing and releasing muscle groups throughout the body to achieve a state of profound relaxation. Starting with the toes and going upward, individuals progressively tension and release each muscle group for a few seconds before moving on to the next.

PMR can assist relieve muscular tension, alleviate physical discomfort, and promote relaxation throughout the body. It can also promote body awareness and mindfulness by focusing attention to sensations and changes in muscular tension.

PMR can be done individually or with the supervision of a qualified therapist or relaxing audio recording. Regular practice can lead to improvements in sleep quality, stress management, and general physical and mental well-being.

By adopting these mindfulness and relaxation practices into their daily routine, individuals may successfully manage stress, increase relaxation, and create better resilience and well-being in their life.

Whether practised separately or in combination, these strategies offer useful tools for handling life's problems with more comfort and serenity.

B. Prioritising Self-Care:

1. Understanding Self-Care:
Self-care refers to purposeful actions and practices that individuals participate in to enhance their physical, mental, and emotional well-being. It entails prioritising one's own needs and taking proactive actions to nourish and refill oneself.

Self-care comprises a wide range of activities, including physical self-care (exercise, diet), emotional self-care (mindfulness, therapy), social self-care (spending time with loved ones, setting boundaries), and spiritual self-care (meditation, introspection).

Prioritising self-care is vital for maintaining balance, resilience, and general well-being, especially in the face of stress, difficulties, and obligations. By attention to their own needs and practising self-compassion, individuals may better cope with life's responsibilities and have a higher quality of life.

2. Practices of Self-Care:
Engaging in activities that provide joy, contentment, and relaxation may serve as a type of self-care. Whether it's pursuing creative hobbies, discovering new interests, or indulging in cherished pleasures, setting aside time for leisure and enjoyment is crucial for nurturing the spirit.

Practising mindfulness and thankfulness can promote self-awareness, reduce stress, and build a stronger feeling of appreciation for life's benefits. Taking moments to pause, think, and relish the present can boost emotional well-being and resilience.

Establishing appropriate limits and saying no to excessive commitments or duties is vital for keeping one's energy and minimising burnout. Learning to prioritise one's own needs and limits is an act of self-respect and self-preservation.

Prioritising physical self-care, such as regular exercise, healthy diet, appropriate sleep, and preventative healthcare, is crucial for sustaining overall health and energy. Taking care of the body creates the basis for maximum well-being and resilience.

Nurturing supportive relationships and building social ties may give crucial sources of emotional support, companionship, and belonging. Spending meaningful time with loved ones, seeking out pleasant social connections, and building a sense of community contribute to general happiness and well-being.

3. Self-Care Rituals:
Incorporating self-care rituals into daily routines can help individuals stay grounded, focused, and balanced throughout life's ups and downs. This may include morning routines, nighttime rituals, or afternoon pauses for rest and renewal.

Taking a holistic approach to self-care means addressing the needs of the mind, body, and spirit. By responding to all elements of their well-being, individuals may find better harmony, resilience, and fulfilment in their life.

Self-care techniques should be adjustable and adjusted to match individual tastes, requirements, and situations. What works for one individual may not work for another, so it's crucial to experiment with different tactics and find what resonates best.

Prioritising self-care is not selfish; it's an essential act of self-preservation and self-compassion. By investing in their personal well-being, individuals may better negotiate life's obstacles, create resilience, and enjoy happier, more satisfying lives.

C. Adequate Rest and Sleep:

1. Understanding Sleep and Stress:
Quality Sleep: Sleep is an essential physiological function that allows the body and mind to relax, mend, and recharge. Quality sleep has a key role in maintaining general health and well-being, including cognitive function, emotional regulation, immunological function, and stress management.

Impact of Stress: Chronic stress can alter sleep patterns and significantly impair sleep quality. Stress drives the body's "fight or flight" response, producing chemicals such as cortisol and adrenaline that can interfere with the sleep-wake cycle and make it difficult to relax and fall asleep.

2. Strategies for Prioritising Sleep:
Consistent Sleep routine: Establishing a consistent sleep routine, where you go to bed and wake up at the same time each day, helps regulate your body's internal clock and enhance sleep quality. Consistency encourages your body's normal sleep-wake cycle, making it simpler to fall asleep and wake up feeling refreshed.

Nighttime ritual: Creating a peaceful nighttime ritual communicates to your body that it's time to wind down and prepare for sleep. This pattern may involve activities like lowering the lights, having a warm bath, practising relaxation techniques like deep breathing or meditation, or reading a book.

Sleep atmosphere: Designing a sleep-conducive atmosphere can boost the quality of your sleep. This involves keeping your bedroom cool, dark, and quiet, investing in a comfortable mattress and pillows, and limiting disturbances such as noise and light pollution. Creating a comfortable and welcoming sleep room can encourage relaxation and help you fall asleep more quickly.

Limiting Stimulants: Avoiding stimulants such as caffeine, nicotine, and electronic gadgets before bedtime will encourage improved sleep quality. Stimulants can interfere with your body's ability to relax and fall asleep, so it's best to avoid them in the hours leading up to bedtime.

Managing Stress: Incorporating stress management practices into your daily routine, such as mindfulness, meditation, yoga, or journaling, can help lower stress levels and promote relaxation, making it easier to fall asleep and stay asleep during the night.

3. Benefits of Adequate Rest and Sleep: Improved Cognitive Function: Quality sleep enhances cognitive function, memory consolidation, and learning. Getting adequate restorative sleep helps you stay awake, focused, and cognitively sharp throughout the day.

Enhanced Mood and Emotional Management: Adequate sleep is vital for emotional well-being and mood management. Sleep deficiency can worsen stress, anxiety, and irritability, whereas sufficient sleep enhances emotional resilience and stability.

Optimised Physical Health: Quality sleep has a crucial role in maintaining immune function, metabolism, and overall physical health. Prioritising sleep can help avoid chronic health issues such as obesity, diabetes, and cardiovascular disease, and enhance lifespan and vitality.

By emphasising adequate rest and sleep, individuals may successfully manage stress, minimise tiredness, and maximise their overall health and well-being. Making sleep a priority and practising regular sleep habits may have substantial advantages for both body and mind, helping you to experience a happier, healthier, and more satisfying life.

By adopting these tactics into their daily routine, individuals may effectively manage stress and exhaustion, increasing their general well-being and reviving their sex life. This proactive approach to self-care creates resilience, promotes relaxation, and cultivates a feeling of balance and harmony throughout midlife and beyond.

3. Seeking Professional Help When Needed:

Sometimes, addressing issues in our sex life may require expert guidance. Whether it's treating underlying medical disorders, investigating psychological difficulties, or seeking direction from a sex therapist, getting professional treatment can give significant support and resources. A trained healthcare professional can give medical therapies for diseases like ED or menopause, while a therapist can assist people and couples overcome emotional or relational difficulties that may be hurting their sexual well-being. By admitting when further assistance is required and being proactive in seeking aid, individuals may overcome hurdles and rejuvenate their sex lives.

1. Recognizing When to Seek Help:
It's vital to identify when issues in our sex life linger despite our efforts to solve them on our own. If difficulties such as erectile dysfunction (ED), menopausal symptoms, marital disputes, or emotional worries continue to influence sexual well-being, obtaining professional treatment may be useful.

Signs that it may be time to seek professional treatment include recurrent challenges with sexual function or enjoyment, feelings of anxiety or discontent linked to sex, or communication breakdowns with your spouse over sexual concerns.

2. Types of Professional Assistance:
Healthcare Providers: Consulting with a healthcare practitioner, such as a primary care physician, urologist, gynaecologist, or endocrinologist, can help detect and treat underlying medical disorders that may be contributing to sexual difficulties. Healthcare practitioners might give medical therapies, such as drugs or hormone therapy, to address difficulties like ED, menopausal symptoms, or other sexual health concerns.

Therapists or Counsellors: Therapists or counsellors specialised in sex therapy or couples therapy can give significant assistance and direction for treating emotional, relational, or psychological aspects influencing sexual well-being. Therapy sessions can help people and couples examine and overcome difficulties such as communication breakdowns, intimacy challenges, sexual trauma, or mental health illnesses like anxiety or depression.

Sex Therapists: Sex therapists are trained specialists that specialise in managing sexual issues and dysfunctions. They can assist people and couples overcome impediments to sexual fulfilment, explore sexual needs and preferences, and develop techniques for boosting closeness and pleasure. Sex therapists offer a secure and nonjudgmental place for addressing sensitive sexual concerns and give evidence-based therapies to improve sexual functioning and well-being.

3. Benefits of Professional Help:
Seeking professional assistance can offer a number of benefits, including:

Expertise and Guidance: Professionals have specific expertise and experience in managing sexual issues and dysfunctions, allowing them to give personalised recommendations and treatments.

Supportive Environment: Therapy sessions give a safe and confidential environment to explore delicate sexual themes, vent problems, and get nonjudgmental support and validation from skilled specialists.

Holistic Approach: Healthcare practitioners and therapists adopt a holistic approach to sexual well-being, treating physical, emotional, relational, and psychological aspects that may contribute to sexual dysfunction. This thorough technique offers holistic healing and long-term sexual enjoyment.

Improved Communication: Professional aid may help people and couples improve communication skills, boost intimacy, and deepen their relationship ties, leading to better sexual satisfaction and fulfilment.

4. Taking the First Step:
Taking the initial step to seek professional treatment may feel frightening, but it's a vital and powerful decision to prioritise your sexual well-being. Start by finding certified healthcare professionals or therapists specialised in sexual health or couples therapy in your region. Reach out to book an initial session to discuss your problems and explore treatment options.

Remember that obtaining professional treatment is a proactive step towards resolving difficulties, enhancing sexual well-being, and reviving your sex life. You deserve to enjoy pleasure, contentment, and fulfilment in your intimate relationships, and expert aid can help you reach these goals.

Chapter Five:

Wellness as a Path to Passion

In the journey towards lively and meaningful intimate relationships, emphasising wellbeing is key. Wellness comprises a comprehensive approach to health, including not just physical well-being but also emotional balance and psychological resiliency. This holistic approach highlights the interdependence of mind, body, and spirit, underlining the enormous influence that each element has on our entire quality of life.

Within the context of intimate relationships, wellness acts as a guiding principle, allowing people and couples the tools and resources to build passion, energy, and connection. Wellness serves as a gateway to passion and happiness in intimate relationships, providing people and couples the tools and resources to create energy, resilience, and connection. By nourishing the body, valuing self-care, and embracing the mind-body connection, individuals may unleash the full potential of their sexual vitality, promoting deeper intimacy, pleasure, and fulfilment in their lives. As we start on our path towards holistic well-being, may we continue to value wellbeing as a cornerstone of lively and meaningful personal relationships.

1. Nourishing the Body for Sexual Vitality:

Nourishing the body creates the framework for sexual health, supplying the critical nutrition and energy needed to power intimate interactions. A balanced diet rich in fruits, vegetables, lean meats, and whole grains supplies the body with the necessary nutrients to maintain general health and well-being. Nutrients such as zinc, vitamin E, and omega-3 fatty acids have been related to increased sexual function and libido, underscoring the relevance of dietary diversification and nutrient sufficiency.

Additionally, staying hydrated and maintaining adequate hydration levels helps enhance blood flow and circulation, crucial variables in sexual desire and responsiveness. Here's a full discussion of how food choices might affect sexual vitality:

1. Balanced Diet: A diet rich in fruits, vegetables, lean meats, and whole grains is the foundation of good health. These foods include critical

vitamins, minerals, antioxidants, and fibre that promote numerous physical processes, including sexual wellness. Consuming a range of nutrient-dense meals ensures that the body obtains all the vital elements it needs to function efficiently.

2. Nutrients for Sexual Health: Certain nutrients have been related to increased sexual function and libido. For example, zinc is necessary for testosterone synthesis and sperm quality in males, while vitamin E functions as an antioxidant that protects against oxidative damage and promotes general reproductive health. Omega-3 fatty acids, found in fatty fish like salmon and flaxseeds, have anti-inflammatory qualities and may enhance blood flow, which is crucial for sexual arousal and responsiveness.

3. Dietary Diversity: Incorporating a wide variety of foods into your diet guarantees that you acquire a broad spectrum of nutrients. Aim to consume a rainbow of fruits and vegetables, as various hues suggest distinct phytonutrients and antioxidants that give diverse health advantages. Including a combination of plant-based and animal-based proteins, such as beans, lentils, tofu, chicken, and fish, guarantees that you

obtain a comprehensive profile of key amino acids needed for muscle repair and hormone synthesis.

4. Hydration: Staying hydrated is vital for general health and well-being, including sexual health. Adequate hydration supports blood flow and circulation, which are necessary for sexual arousal and responsiveness. Drinking water throughout the day helps maintain adequate hydration levels and supports the body's natural processes. Avoiding excessive alcohol use, which can decrease sexual function and desire, is also critical for sustaining sexual vigour.

5. Lifestyle variables: In addition to food, other lifestyle variables play a role in sexual vigour. Regular physical exercise improves cardiovascular health, elevates mood, and raises energy levels, all of which contribute to a healthy sex life. Managing stress with relaxation practices like meditation, deep breathing exercises, or yoga can also promote sexual well-being by lowering tension and fostering relaxation.

Nourishing the body with a balanced diet rich in important nutrients, staying hydrated, and adopting healthy lifestyle practices are crucial components of promoting sexual vigour. By addressing nutritional diversity, nutrient sufficiency, and general well-being, individuals can maximise their sexual health and enjoy rewarding interpersonal interactions.

Regular physical exercise also plays a critical role in promoting sexual vigour. Exercise not only promotes cardiovascular health and stamina but also boosts mood, confidence, and body image - all of which contribute to a good sex life. Engaging in activities that boost heart rate and promote flexibility, such as brisk walking, cycling, or yoga, can enhance physical fitness and sexual performance. Furthermore, getting proper sleep is critical for sexual vitality, as sleep loss can affect hormone balance, emotional management, and cognitive function, all of which affect sexual desire and arousal.

How exercise leads to sexual vitality:

1. Cardiovascular Health: Exercise increases blood circulation and cardiovascular function, which is vital for sexual arousal and performance. By strengthening the heart and boosting blood flow to the genitals, regular physical exercise promotes sexual responsiveness and aids erections in men and lubrication in women.

2. Mood Enhancement: Exercise promotes the production of endorphins, frequently referred to as "feel-good" chemicals, which can boost mood and lessen symptoms of stress, anxiety, and sadness. Improved mood and mental well-being can significantly enhance sexual desire and enjoyment, leading to more gratifying personal interactions.

3. Boosted Confidence: Engaging in regular physical exercise may boost body image, self-esteem, and confidence, all of which are essential variables in sexual attraction and fulfilment. Feeling good about oneself physically and psychologically may lead to better sexual confidence and a more happy sex life.

4. Increased Stamina and Flexibility: Exercise enhances general physical fitness, stamina, and endurance, making it easier to continue sexual activity for longer durations. Additionally, activities that develop flexibility, such as yoga or stretching exercises, can boost range of motion and sexual pleasure, allowing individuals to explore varied positions and motions safely.

5. Hormonal Balance: Adequate physical exercise helps balance hormone levels in the body, including testosterone in males and estrogen in

women. Balanced hormone levels are vital for sustaining sexual desire, arousal, and performance. Regular exercise might help avoid hormonal imbalances that may contribute to sexual dysfunction or low libido.

6. Quality Sleep: Prioritising proper sleep is critical for general health and well-being, including sexual vigour. Sleep deprivation can disturb hormone balance, impede cognitive function, and negatively impact mood, all of which can affect sexual desire and performance. Establishing a consistent sleep schedule and creating a tranquil sleep environment can promote greater sleep quality and enhance sexual health.

Regular physical exercise has a plethora of benefits for sexual vitality, including improved cardiovascular health, greater mood and confidence, increased stamina and flexibility, hormonal balance, and better sleep quality. By adding exercise into their daily routine, individuals may maintain their sexual health and experience a more pleasurable and meaningful sex life.

2. Honouring Self-Care and Holistic Well-Being:

Self-care is the cornerstone of comprehensive well-being, embracing actions that nurture the mind, body, and soul. Honouring self-care requires identifying and prioritising activities that enhance balance, resilience, and vitality. This may involve creating limits to safeguard personal time and energy, participating in relaxing techniques such as meditation or deep breathing exercises, and getting help from loved ones or mental health specialists when required.

Self-care also means participating in activities that provide joy and fulfilment, whether it's spending time in nature, following creative hobbies, or just taking a minute to sip a cup of tea. Here's a full discussion of how respecting self-care adds to overall wellness:

1. Recognizing Priorities: Honouring self-care begins with recognizing and prioritising activities that create balance, resilience, and vitality in our life. This may require creating limits to safeguard personal time and energy, learning to say no to excessive obligations, and prioritising activities that refill our resources and offer us joy.

2. Mindful Relaxation: Engaging in relaxation techniques such as meditation, deep breathing

exercises, or progressive muscle relaxation can help alleviate stress, reduce tension, and create a sense of peace and well-being. These techniques help us to grow mindfulness, anchor ourselves in the present moment, and silence the ceaseless chatter of the mind.

3. Seeking Support: Honouring self-care also means recognizing when we need support and asking out for help from loved ones or mental health specialists. Whether it's talking to a trusted friend, getting therapy, or joining a support group, seeking help may give essential validation, insight, and encouragement during hard times.

4. Indulging in Pleasure: Self-care means indulging in activities that offer us joy, pleasure, and contentment. This might be anything from spending time in nature, indulging in creative hobbies like painting or writing, or simply taking a minute to appreciate a good meal or a relaxing cup of tea. By prioritising things that nourish our souls and raise our spirits, we build a sense of pleasure and fulfilment in our lives.

5. Physical Well-being: Self-care extends to caring for our physical health and well-being. This involves fueling our bodies with good food,

staying hydrated, receiving regular exercise, and having appropriate relaxation and sleep. Taking care of our physical health not only promotes our general well-being but also boosts our resilience and vigour.

6. Emotional and Spiritual Nourishment: Self-care requires catering to our emotional and spiritual needs as well. This may involve practising gratitude, creating positive affirmations, connecting with our inner selves via writing or contemplation, or engaging in spiritual activities such as prayer or meditation. Nurturing our emotional and spiritual well-being develops a sense of inner calm, completeness, and connectedness to something more than ourselves.

Honouring self-care is vital for cultivating comprehensive well-being. By identifying our priorities, participating in mindful relaxation, getting help when required, indulging in pleasure, caring for our physical health, and attention to our emotional and spiritual needs, we create resilience, energy, and a profound feeling of contentment in our life.

Cultivating emotional intelligence and resilience is another vital part of self-care, as it helps individuals to face obstacles and disappointments with grace and compassion. Developing good coping techniques for stress management, such as journaling, practising gratitude, or seeking professional therapy, can promote emotional well-being and build stronger connections in intimate relationships. Additionally, developing social relationships and maintaining a strong support network may give crucial emotional support and validation, boosting overall resilience and well-being.

How growing emotional intelligence and resilience adds to general well-being:

1. Understanding Emotions: Emotional intelligence entails identifying, understanding, and controlling our own emotions as well as empathising with the feelings of others. By growing emotional awareness, we become better able to negotiate the ups and downs of life with greater clarity and insight.

2. Healthy Coping strategies: Developing healthy coping strategies for stress management is a crucial element of self-care. Activities like writing, practising gratitude, or seeking professional therapy can help us manage tough emotions, gain perspective on challenging

situations, and build resilience in the face of adversity.

3. Enhancing Emotional Well-being: Engaging in activities that promote emotional well-being, such as mindfulness meditation, deep breathing exercises, or spending time in nature, may help regulate our emotions and develop a sense of peace and balance. These techniques assist us to create inner calm and tranquillity amidst life's tumult.

4. Fostering Deeper ties: Cultivating emotional intelligence also requires fostering deeper ties in personal relationships. This entails talking freely and honestly with our relationships, demonstrating empathy and understanding, and exercising active listening. By encouraging emotional intimacy and vulnerability, we enhance the connections of trust and connection in our relationships.

5. Social Support Networks: Maintaining a solid support network of family, friends, and community may give vital emotional support and validation during hard times. Having individuals we can turn to for help, encouragement, and friendship boosts our resilience and general well-being.

Cultivating emotional intelligence and resilience is vital for self-care and general well-being. By understanding and controlling our emotions, creating good coping strategies, boosting emotional well-being, fostering deeper connections in relationships, and maintaining a strong support network, we construct the basis for a satisfying and resilient existence.

3. Embracing the Mind-Body Connection:

The mind-body link underlines the interplay between mental and physical health, demonstrating how our ideas, emotions, and beliefs impact our physiological experiences. Embracing the mind-body link requires growing awareness of the ways in which our ideas and emotions affect our physical well-being, particularly in the domain of sexuality and intimacy. Mindfulness activities, such as meditation, yoga, or breathwork, can assist individuals improve present-moment awareness and sensitivity to physiological sensations, boosting pleasure and closeness in sexual interactions.

How appreciating the mind-body link helps to sexual well-being:

1. Awareness of Thoughts and feelings:
Cultivating awareness of our thoughts, feelings, and beliefs helps us to realise how they impact our bodily experiences, including sexuality. For example, negative thoughts or stress might emerge as bodily tightness or impede sexual desire. By becoming attentive of our mental and emotional states, we may recognize and overcome impediments to sexual pleasure and closeness.

2. Practising Mindfulness: Mindfulness activities, such as meditation, yoga, or breathwork, are helpful tools for improving present-moment awareness and sensitivity to physiological sensations. These activities assist individuals quiet the mind, reduce tension, and boost sensitivity to physical touch, resulting in greater enjoyment and closeness in sexual relationships.

3. Addressing Performance Anxiety: Performance anxiety, or worry of not fulfilling sexual expectations, is a prevalent issue that can limit sexual fulfilment. By exercising mindfulness practices, individuals can learn to notice and accept their thoughts and feelings without judgement, lowering anxiety and encouraging calm during sexual activity.

4. Enhancing Sensual Awareness: Mindfulness enables individuals to participate completely in sensory experiences, especially those connected to sexuality. By paying attention to the sensations of touch, taste, smell, and sound during sexual experiences, individuals may improve their connection with their partners and heighten pleasure and closeness.

5. Integrating Mind and Body: Embracing the mind-body link means acknowledging that our physical health and well-being are interwoven with our mental and emotional emotions. By emphasising self-care, reducing stress, and fostering good thoughts and emotions, individuals may create an ideal environment for sexual vitality and pleasure.

Embracing the mind-body link in sexuality entails fostering awareness of how our ideas, emotions, and feelings affect our physical experiences. Through mindfulness techniques, reducing performance anxiety, expanding sensory awareness, and integrating mind and body, individuals can increase pleasure, closeness, and satisfaction in their sexual interactions. Exploring the importance of pleasure and sensuality in daily life is another crucial component of accepting the mind-body connection. Cultivating an appreciation for the sensuous pleasures of life – whether it's indulging in a good meal, luxuriating in a warm bath, or savouring the touch of a loved one – may increase general well-being and energy. Additionally, resolving any psychological hurdles or traumas that may inhibit sexual expression is vital for enjoying the mind-body connection fully. Seeking professional therapy or counselling may give a safe environment to examine and heal old hurts, helping individuals to create a greater sense of self-awareness and sexual empowerment. Here's how it adds to general well-being:

1. Appreciating Sensual joys: Cultivating an appreciation for the sensual joys of everyday life can increase our connection to the present moment and generate a sense of energy. Taking time to indulge in activities that engage the senses – such as savouring a wonderful meal, listening to music, or bathing in nature's beauty - may improve mood, reduce stress, and develop a deeper connection with ourselves and our environment.

2. Nurturing Intimate Relationships: Sensuality extends beyond physical contact and may embrace emotional closeness and connection

with loved ones. Engaging in activities that create emotional connection – such as sincere talks, acts of generosity, or spending quality time together – deepens bonds and boosts overall pleasure in relationships.

3. Healing Psychological obstacles: Addressing psychological obstacles or traumas that restrict sexual expression is vital for enjoying the mind-body connection completely. Seeking therapy or counselling gives a safe and supportive place to explore previous wounds, confront harmful beliefs, and establish better patterns of thinking and conduct. By addressing underlying issues, individuals may create a greater sense of self-awareness, heal emotional traumas, and recover their sexual empowerment.

4. Cultivating Self-Awareness: Exploring pleasure and sensuality builds self-awareness and self-acceptance, allowing individuals to embrace their desires, preferences, and limits without condemnation. By tuning into our bodies' cues and honouring our wants and desires, we may create a stronger feeling of authenticity, confidence, and empowerment in our sexual experiences.

Embracing pleasure and sensuality in daily life strengthens our connection to ourselves, our relationships, and the world around us. By strengthening personal connections, removing psychological obstacles, and growing self-awareness, individuals may fully embrace the mind-body link and feel increased contentment, vitality, and sexual empowerment.

Chapter Six:

Pleasure Playgrounds: Exploring New Territories

As individuals hit their 40s and beyond, they frequently find themselves at a unique juncture in their life, where the quest of pleasure takes on a new dimension. This stage is a time of self-discovery, where one's sense of identity and desires grow more refined and prominent. It's a stage defined by a greater awareness of oneself and a developing appreciation for the numerous feelings and experiences life has to offer.

In this journey of inquiry, sensual enjoyment takes centre stage. From the delicate caress of a loved one's hand to the taste of great cuisine, every feeling is appreciated with heightened awareness and appreciation. The senses become doorways to a world of pleasure, enabling individuals to explore and relish in the richness of their experiences.

But the hunt for pleasure stretches beyond the bounds of the familiar bedroom. It surpasses customary bounds and delves into unexplored territory, enjoying the excitement of sensual escapades in unexpected settings. Whether it's a surprise rendezvous under the stars or a covert tryst in a secret nook, the attraction of novelty and spontaneity adds a thrilling depth to personal relationships.

Yet, at its root, the journey of pleasure is about more than simply bodily feelings. It's about tapping into new areas of pleasure that go beyond the surface, digging into the depths of one's passions and dreams. It's about accepting authenticity and enjoying the inherent quirks and eccentricities that make each individual's path of pleasure distinctly their own.

In this exploration of new areas, individuals are asked to lose inhibitions and embrace the whole range of their desires. It's a voyage of self-discovery and self-expression, where each moment is an opportunity to relish in the joy of being alive and the endless possibilities that await. So, let's go on this voyage together, exploring the landscape of pleasure with curiosity, enthusiasm, and a sense of wonder.

1. Sensory Exploration and Heightened Sensations

Sensory exploration and heightened feelings are at the heart of unlocking new layers of pleasure and connection, especially as individuals develop into their 40s and beyond. This era of life frequently carries with it a better understanding for the subtle subtleties of sensory experiences, as well as a desire to explore and enjoy them more thoroughly.

One component of sensory exploration entails tuning into the five senses - sight, hearing, taste, touch, and smell – and allowing them to steer the journey of intimacy. For example, lowering the lights and establishing a soft, ambient ambiance can boost visual stimulation, allowing partners to focus on each other's bodies and motions. Similarly, integrating sensuous music or ambient noises can heighten auditory feelings, providing a degree of intimacy and connection to the encounter.

Sensory exploration includes purposefully activating and increasing each of the five senses during intimate times to enhance the overall experience. Here's a summary of how each sensation may be studied in detail:

1. Sight: Visual stimulus plays a vital role in sensory exploration. Dimming the lights or utilising candles may create a calm and romantic air, creating the tone for intimacy. Additionally, integrating visually attractive items such as luxury fabrics, beautiful lingerie, or sensuous décor may improve the visual experience and induce emotions of want and arousal.

2. Hearing: Auditory stimuli can also contribute to sensory exploration. Playing quiet, seductive music in the background or listening to the sound of each other's breathing and murmurs may heighten the closeness of the moment. The rhythmic sound of bodies moving together or the exchange of murmured endearments can improve the sensuous experience and increase emotional connection.

3. Taste: Exploring taste sensations may bring an added element of intensity to sexual relationships. Sharing tasty goodies like chocolate-covered strawberries or feeding each other fruits may excite the taste senses and create a joyful and sexual encounter. Experimenting with diverse flavours and textures may excite the senses and make the experience more delightful and memorable.

4. Touch: Touch is possibly the most vital sense when it comes to intimacy. Sensual caresses, delicate massages, and exploring each other's body with light touches may produce a profound sense of connection and pleasure. Experimenting with varied textures, temperatures, and pressures can heighten feelings and boost enjoyment. Additionally, integrating sensuous objects like feathers, silk scarves, or massage oils may bring variety and excitement to tactile exploration.

5. Smell: Scents may trigger intense emotions and memories, making them a vital element of sensory investigation. Lighting fragrant candles or utilising essential oils with aphrodisiac characteristics like jasmine, vanilla, or ylang-ylang may create a sensuous and appealing atmosphere. The delicate interplay of smells can increase relaxation, heighten arousal, and deepen closeness during intimate times.

By actively engaging and stimulating each of the five senses, partners may create a multi-dimensional and immersive experience that heightens pleasure, deepens emotional connection, and encourages intimacy and closeness in their relationship.

Taste also plays a crucial part in sensory exploration, since indulging in delectable meals and beverages may awaken the palate and engage the senses. Experimenting with aphrodisiac foods or sharing a sensuous dinner together may generate a shared sensation of pleasure and arousal. Additionally, introducing fun activities like feeding each other chocolate-covered strawberries or sharing a glass of wine may lend a sense of romance and sensuality to the occasion.

Taste offers additional level to sensory exploration during intimate moments. Indulging in delectable foods and beverages together may create a unique and unforgettable experience. Here's how taste may boost sensory exploration:

1. Aphrodisiac meals: Some meals are said to have aphrodisiac effects, meaning they can stimulate sexual desire or arousal. Experimenting with aphrodisiac foods like oysters, strawberries, avocado, and dark chocolate may heighten senses and create a sexual atmosphere.

2. Sensuous Meals: Sharing a sensuous meal together may be an intimate and connecting experience. Cooking together or dining at a romantic restaurant allows couples to relish each

mouthful and enjoy the flavours and textures of the cuisine. Taking the time to savour the culinary experience may excite the senses and increase the overall mood.

3. Playful Activities: Incorporating playful activities like feeding each other morsels of food or sharing a bottle of wine may bring an element of pleasure and excitement to the sensory investigation. It encourages partners to let go of inhibitions and accept the present, generating a sense of closeness and connection.

By combining taste into sensory exploration, partners may create a rich and rewarding encounter that tantalises the palate and stimulates passion and desire.

Of course, touch is arguably the most vital sense when it comes to closeness and pleasure. Sensory exploration through touch entails employing diverse textures, tensions, and strategies to produce heightened feelings and arousal. This might involve delicate caresses, forceful massages, feather-light touches, or even investigating the use of silk scarves or feathers to stimulate the skin and activate the nerve endings.

Indeed, contact is crucial to closeness and enjoyment. Exploring feelings through touch may be immensely gratifying and fulfilling. Here's how sensory exploration through touch works:

1. Varied Textures: Incorporating diverse textures may increase tactile impressions and offer a more exciting experience. Experiment with soft textiles like silk or velvet, smooth surfaces like satin sheets, or rough textures like a loofah or massage tool. Each texture delivers a distinct experience that can heighten arousal and enjoyment.

2. Pressure and Technique: Varying the pressure and technique of touch provides depth and variety to sensory inquiry. Gentle caresses, strong massages, or fun tickles can provoke varied experiences and responses in the body. Pay attention to your partner's emotions and alter your touch properly to enhance enjoyment.

3. Sensory instruments: Utilising sensory instruments like silk scarves, feathers, or massage oils may intensify tactile sensations and make the experience more immersive. Experiment with different tools and strategies to discover what feels best for you and your spouse.

Incorporating sensory items adds a sense of freshness and excitement to intimate times.

By exploring feelings via touch, couples may strengthen their connection and increase their physical and emotional closeness. Taking the time to engage in sensory exploration may lead to heightened arousal, improved pleasure, and a stronger sense of closeness and connection between couples.

Furthermore, engaging the sense of scent may also increase the sensation of closeness and pleasure. Aromatherapy oils, scented candles, or aromatic flowers can be introduced into the surroundings to create an atmosphere of relaxation and sensuality. Certain aromas, such as lavender or jasmine, are recognized for their relaxing and aphrodisiac characteristics, making them excellent for setting the tone for intimacy.

The sense of scent may substantially impact the whole sensation of closeness and pleasure. Here's how combining aroma into sensory inquiry may enhance the moment:

1. Aromatherapy Oils: Aromatherapy oils, such as lavender, rose, or sandalwood, can inspire sensations of relaxation, desire, and sensuality.

Diffusing these oils in the air or applying them straight to the skin during massage can produce a calming and inviting atmosphere for intimacy.

2. Scented Candles: Lighting scented candles with smells like vanilla, jasmine, or ylang-ylang may give warmth and atmosphere to the space. The warm glow of candlelight paired with the faint perfume of the candles may heighten the senses and create a romantic and intimate ambiance.

3. Fragrant Flowers: Fresh flowers like roses, lilies, or orchids not only give beauty to the area but also fill the air with their natural aroma. Placing a bouquet of aromatic flowers in the room may stimulate the senses and set the mood for closeness.

4. Unique Smells: Experimenting with unique smells, such as pheromone-infused perfumes or colognes, can lend an air of surprise and fascination to sexual interactions. These smells are meant to promote attraction and inspire desire, making them a pleasant and engaging complement to sensory exploration.

Incorporating fragrance into sensory exploration may heighten arousal, trigger emotional reactions, and create a more immersive and lasting experience of intimacy. Whether through aromatherapy oils, scented candles, or fragrant flowers, cultivating the sense of smell may give depth and richness to intimate times between lovers.

Sensory exploration and heightened feelings include embracing the whole gamut of sensory experiences to improve closeness and enjoyment. By tuning into the senses and letting them direct the journey of intimacy, individuals may open new dimensions of pleasure and connection with their partners, deepening their relationships and boosting their overall well-being.

2. Erotic Adventures Beyond the Bedroom

Exploring erotic adventures outside the bedroom means venturing beyond standard sexual settings and embracing new places, activities, and experiences that kindle desire and excitement. Here's a full study of this concept:

1. Outdoor Adventures: Taking intimacy outside may give a feeling of excitement and spontaneity to your sexual experiences. Whether it's a quiet beach, a lush forest, or a picturesque overlook,

outdoor locations give seclusion and the opportunity to connect with nature while exploring your fantasies together.

Exploring intimacy outdoors involves choosing private areas in nature, like a calm beach, a serene forest, or a magnificent view point, where you and your spouse may enjoy each other's company away from the rush and bustle of regular life. Being surrounded by nature may make your encounters feel more special and exciting, and it creates a sense of seclusion that allows you to focus on each other without interruptions. Whether it's watching the sunset together, feeling the breeze on your skin, or listening to the sounds of birds singing, being outside may heighten your senses and make your personal moments even more unforgettable.

2. Role-Playing and Fantasy Exploration: Embracing role-playing scenarios and exploring sexual fantasies may offer an element of surprise and excitement to your sensual encounters. Dressing up in costumes, assuming different characters, and inventing intricate scenarios allows you to release your creativity and revel in new experiences together.

Role-playing is pretending to be someone else or taking on a new role in a sexual encounter. It's like acting out a scene from a movie or a narrative, but with your partner. For example, you might pretend to be strangers meeting for the first time at a pub, or you could act out a dream where one of you is a mischievous student and the other is the severe teacher. Role-playing allows you to explore other parts of themselves and engage in fantasies that you might not feel comfortable expressing in your regular lives. It adds an element of excitement and adventure to your sex life, making your experiences more fun and gratifying.

3. Sensory Experiences: Engaging in sensory experiences that engage the senses can heighten arousal and deepen closeness. This can involve activities like blindfolded massage, sensuous food tasting, or playing with temperature play with icy or heated oils. By focusing on sensory stimulation, you may strengthen your connection and experience new dimensions of pleasure.

Sensory experiences entail using diverse sensations like touch, taste, and temperature to improve closeness and enjoyment. For example, you may try blindfolding your lover and giving them a massage, depending purely on touch to develop anticipation and excitement. You might even explore food by feeding each other fruits or chocolates, savouring the flavour and texture together. Another possibility is to play with temperature, such as using ice cubes or heated oils during massage to produce contrasting sensations on the skin. These sensory experiences can heighten arousal and make your personal encounters more thrilling and gratifying.

4. Travel and Exploration: Embarking on romantic vacations or travel excursions gives the perfect opportunity to explore your sexuality in new and exotic locales. Whether it's a weekend vacation to a lovely cabin in the woods or an exciting journey to a foreign place, travel allows you to break free from routine and immerse yourselves in new experiences that inspire passion and desire.

Travelling together to new and fascinating areas may spice up your sex life by providing a sense of adventure and spontaneity. Imagine retiring to a secluded lodge in the woods or experiencing a lively metropolis together. Being in an unfamiliar location may activate your senses and encourage closeness. Plus, attempting new hobbies or experiencing local culture may bring you closer together as you share new experiences and make lasting memories. Whether it's a romantic weekend break or an exciting vacation overseas, travel brings up unlimited options for sensual pleasures outside the bedroom.

5. Public Play and Exhibitionism: For individuals who prefer a sense of excitement, engaging in public play or exhibitionism may be an amazing way to spice up your erotic encounters. This could entail gently caressing or teasing each other in public areas, such as a crowded restaurant or a movie theatre, or participating in more risky actions in semi-public locales.

Engaging in public play or exhibitionism may bring an extra thrill to your sex life by providing an element of danger and excitement. Picture quietly tormenting each other in a busy restaurant or sneaking kisses in a dark movie theatre. It's about finding covert methods to explore your needs in public places, knowing that you're sharing a secret intimacy amidst the hustle and bustle of ordinary life. For those feeling more brave, semi-public venues like isolated parks or vacant stairwells give the possibility to indulge in more risky behaviours while preserving an aspect of concealment. Just be careful to emphasise consent and respect for others' limits when experiencing this wonderful facet of sexual adventure.

6. Erotic Art and Culture: Exploring erotic art, literature, and cultural events may inspire new ideas and dreams while enhancing your awareness for sexuality and sensuality. Visiting art galleries, seeing burlesque acts, or reading sensual literature together may generate conversation and fuel passion, establishing a stronger connection between couples.

Engaging with erotic art, literature, and cultural events may be a rewarding way to explore your sexuality and strengthen your connection with your spouse. Imagine going through an art gallery, admiring seductive paintings and sculptures that provoke desire and passion. Or watching a captivating burlesque show, where performers enchant with their seductive moves and charm. Reading sexy books together may kindle your imagination and generate important talks about desires and dreams. By immersing yourselves in the realm of erotic art and culture, you not only extend your sexual horizons but also enhance your relationship as a pair via shared experiences and shared wants.

By enjoying sensual adventures beyond the bedroom, couples can discover new channels for closeness, passion, and pleasure. Whether via outdoor excursions, role-playing fantasies, sensuous encounters, or cultural inquiry, moving outside of the bedroom helps partners to break away from monotony and unlock new layers of their sexuality.

3. Tapping into New Realms of Pleasure

Tapping into new levels of pleasure means researching unique and inventive methods to feel pleasure and closeness. It's about pushing limits, trying new things, and broadening your awareness of what brings you and your partner happiness. Here are some techniques to go into new regions of pleasure:

1. Sensory Deprivation: Experimenting with sensory deprivation techniques, such as blindfolding or wearing earplugs, can heighten your other senses and increase experiences.

Sensory deprivation is like turning down the volume on certain of your senses to make others louder. For example, consider blindfolding oneself or wearing earplugs. When you do this, your other sensations, including touch, taste, and smell, get stronger because you're paying more attention to them. So, when you touch or taste anything during intimacy, it seems much more intense and thrilling since you're focused on it more. This may make the encounter feel deeper and more immersive, providing a new dimension of enjoyment to your private times.

2. Tantric Practices: Delve into the ancient discipline of Tantra, which stresses awareness, breathwork, and sensual contact to generate heightened states of arousal and pleasure. Tantra is like a specific method of connecting with your spouse during intimate moments. It's all about slowing down, paying attention to your breath, and focusing on each other's bodies in a thoughtful way. By doing this, you can feel more connected and in sync with each other, both physically and emotionally. Tantra can develop a deeper feeling of pleasure and closeness, making your time together even more precious and meaningful.

3. Conscious Kink: Explore the realm of conscious kink, where BDSM activities are handled with mindfulness, communication, and permission at the forefront. Engaging in power play, bondage, or sensation play may unleash new layers of pleasure and vulnerability, enabling

you to explore different elements of your desires and fantasies in a safe and consenting manner.

Conscious kink is like pursuing daring and sometimes edgy behaviours with your partner, but in a conscious and respectful way. It entails good communication and making sure both couples are comfortable and agree to everything. So, whether it's trying out role-playing, utilising handcuffs, or experimenting with new sensations, it's all about having fun while being conscious of each other's boundaries and wants.

4. Sensual Massage: Take your massage sessions to the next level by including sensual methods and seductive touches. Explore erogenous zones, try with varied pressures and strokes, and use exquisite oils or lotions to heighten arousal and relaxation. Erotic massage not only feels wonderful but also encourages closeness and connection between lovers.

Erotic massage is like normal massage, but with a seductive twist! You and your lover may explore each other's bodies in a sensuous way, utilising soft touches and specific oils to increase enjoyment. It's a terrific way to relax together and establish closeness while also ramping up the heat in the bedroom. Just be sure to communicate and take it gently to guarantee a pleasant and happy experience for both of you.

5. Sexual Exploration Games: Spice up your bedroom routine with sexual exploration games or activities meant to promote curiosity and inventiveness. Whether it's a deck of sensual cards, a dirty board game, or a digital app, these games give a lighthearted approach to uncover new desires, preferences, and limits while having fun with your partner.

Sexual exploration games are like playing games, but with a sensual twist! You and your lover might try out different games or challenges that allow you to explore your wants and dreams together. It's a fun and lighthearted approach to spice up your personal encounters and discover more about each other's turn-ons. Just remember to make everything consensual and courteous, and have fun discovering new things together!

6. Sacred Sexuality Rituals: Incorporate sacred sexuality rituals into your personal relationships to infuse them with meaning, intention, and spiritual connection. This might entail creating a holy place, making intentions, and engaging in rituals like eye gazing, breathwork, or meditation

to deepen your connection and boost enjoyment on a fundamental level.

Sacred sexuality rituals are like unique ceremonies you and your spouse may develop to make your intimate times even more meaningful and spiritual. You may set up a beautiful environment with candles and quiet music, then spend some time connecting with each other through eye contact, deep breathing, or meditation. These rituals can help you feel more connected and present with each other, boosting the joy and intimacy of your encounter.

By tapping into new regions of pleasure, you and your lover may begin on an exhilarating voyage of exploration, discovery, and satisfaction. Remember to talk clearly, emphasise consent, and approach each new encounter with curiosity and respect for each other's wishes and boundaries.

Chapter Seven:

Tech Tools for Erotic Enhancement

In today's digital era, technology has transformed all areas of our life, including our personal encounters and relationships. From inventive equipment meant to improve pleasure to digital platforms that encourage personal encounters, technology provides a plethora of instruments for sexual enhancement. In this chapter, we will look at how individuals might use technology for pleasure, dig into the domain of digital intimacy and connection, and find the ways in which innovation can be easily interwoven into intimate interactions. Read on as we go on a tour into the fascinating world of digital tools for sensual improvement.

1. Harnessing Technology for Pleasure

Harnessing technology for pleasure means employing numerous equipment, gadgets, and programs to enhance our personal encounters and sexual enjoyment. In today's digital era, there is a vast range of technical developments intended expressly for this purpose. These gadgets might range from basic vibrating devices to complex software and virtual reality experiences.

Some of the ways in which technology might be exploited for pleasure include:

1. Sex Toys: Sex toys are equipment meant to make sex more exciting. They come in different sorts, such vibrators for ladies, dildos, and toys for males. These toys may be used alone or with a partner to offer added thrill and pleasure to intimate moments. They come in varied shapes, sizes, and functions, so there's something for everyone's interests and preferences. Whether it's adding a buzz with a vibrator or trying out new sensations with a dildo, sex toys can spice up your sex life and make things more exciting and rewarding.

2. App-Controlled Devices: Some sex toys may be controlled via smartphone applications. These toys include Bluetooth or Wi-Fi connections, so you can control them from your phone. This means you or your spouse may modify the settings or strength of the toy's vibrations without being immediately next to one other. It provides a touch of excitement and surprise to long-distance relationships or even just to spice things up in the bedroom.

3. Virtual Reality (VR): Virtual reality (VR) technology allows users to have authentic sexual experiences in virtual worlds. With VR headsets, users may immerse themselves in realistic environments and explore their imaginations. It's like entering into a separate universe where you may connect with virtual companions or discover new activities without any real-world implications.

4. Online Platforms and Communities: Online platforms and communities give a space for people to explore their sexuality and interact with others who share similar interests. These platforms can include websites for erotic literature, forums for debate, and social media networks focusing on adult material. By joining these groups, individuals may share experiences, seek guidance, and discover new methods to explore their interests in a helpful and non-judgmental atmosphere.

5. Sexual Health Apps: Indeed, technology may be a helpful tool for boosting sexual health and well-being. There are applications aimed to teach users about sexual health subjects such as STIs, contraception, and reproductive health. These applications give factual information and resources to help users make educated decisions

regarding their sexual health. Additionally, several applications include tools that allow users to track their sexual behaviour, menstrual cycles, and contraceptive use, helping them keep organised and educated about their reproductive health. Furthermore, there are applications that give guided exercises and strategies for boosting sexual pleasure and intimacy, enabling individuals explore new ways to connect with their partners and increase their overall sexual happiness.

Harnessing technology for pleasure provides unlimited opportunities for enriching our personal encounters and exploring our sexual urges. Whether via the use of sex toys, virtual reality experiences, or online platforms, technology has the potential to transform the way we interact with our sexuality and connect with others in the digital age.

2. Exploring Digital Intimacy and Connection

Exploring digital intimacy and connection entails utilising technology to promote emotional closeness and intimacy between couples, especially in long-distance relationships or during times of physical separation.

Some ways in which digital platforms and applications may foster intimacy:

1. Video Calls and Messaging applications: Video calls and messaging applications have altered how couples interact and connect, especially while they're physically separated. Platforms like Skype, FaceTime, WhatsApp, and Zoom enable partners to engage in real-time, regardless of their physical location. Through video conversations, couples may see each other's facial expressions, hear their voices, and share experiences as if they were together in person. This visual and aural connection helps bridge the physical gap and builds emotional closeness between lovers.

These applications give a forum for couples to participate in meaningful discussions, communicate updates about their day, and show affection via words and actions. Whether it's a brief check-in during a lunch break or a lengthier talk before bedtime, video calls and messaging applications allow couples to stay connected throughout the day. Seeing each other's smiles, laughing, and demonstrations of affection increases the emotional tie between spouses and promotes their sense of togetherness.

Moreover, these platforms provide numerous features like audio messaging, stickers, and emoticons, which enhance communication and make it more expressive and engaging. Couples may exchange spontaneous messages, share photographs and videos, or even play interactive games together, adding fun and excitement to their interactions.

Video conversations and messaging applications have become crucial tools for sustaining intimacy and connection in long-distance relationships or during times of physical separation. They give couples with a handy and accessible method to stay connected, share experiences, and develop their love, regardless of the miles that

2. Virtual Date Nights: Virtual date nights have arisen as an innovative method for couples to spend quality time together and enhance their relationship, even when they're miles apart. Through video conversations, couples may organise and participate in numerous activities that imitate the sensation of being on a typical date.

One popular virtual date concept is making supper together over video call. Couples may pick a recipe, gather ingredients, then follow along with each other while they create the dinner. This collaborative culinary experience not only develops a sense of collaboration but also allows couples to partake in the satisfaction of producing something tasty together.

Another option for virtual date evenings is viewing a movie or TV show concurrently while video calling. Couples may pick a movie, hit play at the same moment, and then watch and respond to the film together in real-time. This shared viewing experience allows couples to enjoy each other's companionship while indulging in their favourite entertainment.

For couples who love a little friendly rivalry, internet games give a wonderful opportunity for virtual date evenings. Whether it's a multiplayer video game, an online trivia quiz, or a virtual escape room, playing games together over video chat can be a fun and engaging way to bond and create memorable memories.

Virtual date evenings allow couples the option to interact and share experiences, despite being physically apart. By engaging in activities together over video call, couples may deepen their relationship, establish intimacy, and create meaningful connections that transcend distance.

3. Sending Digital Presents and Surprises:
Sending digital presents and surprises is a
considerate way for couples to demonstrate love
and gratitude, even while they're separated. With
the convenience of technology, couples may
effortlessly send virtual presents and surprises to
one other, brightening each other's day and
increasing their emotional connection.

One popular digital gift choice is sending e-cards.
These electronic greeting cards may be
customised with unique words and designs,
making them a sincere way to convey love and
compassion. Whether it's a romantic greeting, a
hilarious meme, or a sweet animation, e-cards
may transmit a range of feelings and ideas.

Virtual flowers are another popular alternative for
digital gifting. With only a few clicks, couples can
send each other virtual bouquets of flowers,
replete with brilliant hues and fragrant blossoms.
While they may not have the same aroma as
actual flowers, virtual bouquets may nonetheless
offer joy and beauty to the recipient's day.

Personalised playlists are a unique way to convey
love and attention via music. Partners can
construct playlists of their favourite songs,
personal experiences, or important lyrics, and

share them with one other via streaming platforms or digital music services. Listening to these playlists can trigger shared memories and feelings, enhancing the emotional connection between lovers.

In addition to digital presents, unexpected words and gestures given via email or social media may also make partners feel cherished and appreciated. Whether it's a poignant letter, a hilarious joke, or a sweet GIF, unexpected surprises from a loved one may brighten even the darkest days and enhance the link between couples.

Sending digital presents and surprises is a simple yet significant method for couples to nourish their relationship and demonstrate love and respect for one other, even while they're physically separated. With the power of technology, couples can stay connected and express their sentiments in imaginative and emotional ways, no matter the distance.

4. Online Relationship Therapy: Online relationship therapy provides couples with a simple and accessible alternative to address difficulties and develop their connection. Through virtual therapy sessions performed via video

conferences, couples may get advice and support from experienced therapists without the need to attend a physical location.

One of the key benefits of online relationship therapy is its accessibility. Couples can attend therapy sessions from the comfort of their own home, reducing the need for travel and making it easier to organise appointments around hectic schedules. This convenience makes it simpler for couples to prioritise their relationship and commit to the therapy process.

Another advantage of internet therapy is its flexibility. With virtual therapy sessions, couples have the flexibility to pick from a larger pool of therapists who may specialise in their unique needs or preferences. Additionally, online therapy offers more flexible scheduling possibilities, allowing couples to select appointment times that suit both spouses.

Online relationship therapy also offers couples with a secure and confidential venue to confront sensitive problems and work through obstacles. Through guided talks and therapy procedures, couples may examine their feelings, enhance communication, and create ways for resolving issues constructively. The presence of a skilled therapist guarantees that both couples feel heard and supported during the therapy session.

Furthermore, online relationship therapy may be particularly useful for couples in long-distance relationships or those confronting geographical restrictions. By employing video chats, couples may engage in therapy sessions together regardless of their physical location, allowing them to work on their relationship and conquer challenges together.

Online relationship therapy gives couples a convenient, flexible, and effective approach to enhance their bond, increase communication, and resolve disputes. With the advice of a qualified therapist, couples may manage problems, develop their emotional connection, and establish a better and more rewarding relationship.

5. Sharing Digital Memories: Sharing digital memories is a genuine method for couples to cherish important moments and celebrate their love journey. Through images, videos, and online journals, couples may create a digital library of memories that record their love, progress, and travels together.

One of the advantages of sharing digital memories is the simplicity and convenience of preserving significant occurrences. With smartphones and digital cameras, couples can record spontaneous experiences in an instant, whether it's a romantic date night, a picturesque getaway, or a nice night in. These images and films offer physical memories of the love and joy exchanged between spouses.

Additionally, digital memories may be conveniently managed and retrieved through many internet platforms and apps. Couples may establish shared albums or online diaries where they can post and save their images and videos, making it simple to return and relive precious experiences together. This accessibility allows couples to reminisce about their experiences and build their emotional connection, even while they're physically separated.

Sharing digital memories also develops a sense of closeness and connection between spouses. By exchanging images, videos, and messages, couples can stay connected throughout the day and engage in one other's life, no matter where they are. This regular conversation and sharing of experiences build the emotional link between spouses and reaffirm their devotion to each other.

Moreover, digital memories serve as a source of comfort and nostalgia, especially during times of separation or difficulties. Revisiting shared experiences may elicit feelings of warmth and contentment, reminding couples of the love and support they have for each other. Whether it's flicking through old photographs or viewing movies from memorable situations, digital memories make couples feel closer and more connected, even while they're physically separated.

Sharing digital memories is a significant way for couples to celebrate their love, develop enduring relationships, and enhance their relationship over time. By documenting and preserving great moments together, couples may develop a treasure trove of memories that will continue to bring them joy and connection for years to come.

6. Engaging in Virtual Intimacy: Engaging in virtual intimacy provides couples a method to retain emotional and sexual connection, regardless of physical distance. While physical contact is frequently linked with intimacy, virtual

means may nevertheless build connection and enjoyment between lovers.

One method couples might participate in virtual intimacy is through personal messaging. Sending sincere messages, expressing wants, or discussing dreams may build a sense of emotional connection and anticipation. These messages allow couples to convey their thoughts and wishes, keeping the flame alive even while they're away.

Phone or video sex is another option for couples to explore virtual intimacy. Through phone conversations or video chats, partners can participate in sexual acts together, such as mutual masturbation or verbal seduction. These intimate interactions allow couples to feel pleasure and arousal in real-time, while being physically apart.

Interactive sex gadgets connected via the internet give yet another outlet for virtual connection. Couples may use app-controlled sex gadgets to excite one other from a distance, improving sexual pleasure and intimacy. These devices allow lovers to enjoy intimate encounters and discover new sensations together, regardless of their geographical location.

Engaging in virtual intimacy helps couples to retain sexual connection and pleasure, even when they can't be together in person. By embracing technology and creativity, couples may continue to cultivate their relationship and enjoy rewarding personal moments, no matter the distance.

Exploring digital intimacy and connection entails harnessing technology to build emotional closeness, sustain communication, and cultivate the link between lovers, regardless of physical distance or circumstances. By creatively leveraging digital tools and platforms, couples may create a strong and resilient relationship that lives on intimacy and connection.

3. Integrating Innovation into Intimate Experiences

Integrating innovation into personal interactions entails combining cutting-edge technology, current methodologies, and creative ways to promote enjoyment, connection, and happiness in relationships. By embracing innovation, couples may discover fascinating and dynamic ways to enhance intimacy and create amazing moments together, ushering in a new era of sexual exploration and pleasure.

Advanced sex toys and gadgets provide a novel way to improve intimate interactions between lovers. These gadgets are loaded with cutting-edge features and capabilities, painstakingly engineered to increase sexual pleasure and satisfaction to unparalleled heights. With a varied choice of alternatives available, couples have the chance to go on an amazing voyage of adventure and discovery together.

One fascinating element of sophisticated sex gadgets is their capacity to link lovers across distances. App-controlled vibrators, for example, enable users to remotely manage the device's settings and intensity levels, allowing for intimate play and contact even while separated by physical distance. This revolutionary feature not only develops a sense of closeness and connection but also adds an element of excitement and anticipation to sexual experiences.

Furthermore, the development of advanced robotic gadgets has altered the terrain of sexual stimulation. These state-of-the-art gadgets are meant to imitate the feelings of human touch with incredible accuracy and precision. From accurate textures to configurable settings, these gadgets offer a completely immersive and luxurious experience for consumers. Couples may discover new worlds of pleasure and stimulation together, stretching the boundaries of intimacy and connection in the process.

Moreover, modern sex toys and gadgets give couples a wealth of possibilities to spice up their sexual repertoire. With features like different vibration patterns, adjustable intensity levels, and customised settings, these gadgets provide unlimited options for experimentation and discovery. Whether seeking moderate stimulation or powerful sensations, couples may adjust their experience to fit their preferences and needs, creating unforgettable and amazing moments together.

Advanced sex toys and gadgets reflect a paradigm change in the way couples approach intimacy and pleasure. By adopting these modern technologies, couples may unleash new layers of pleasure, excitement, and connection in their sexual interactions. From remote play to lifelike simulations, these gadgets give up a world of possibilities for couples to explore, strengthening their relationship and promoting a greater feeling of closeness and pleasure.

Incorporating novel approaches and practices into intimate encounters may breathe fresh life into the bedroom and revive love between couples. One such way is tantric sex, a centuries-old discipline that focuses on awareness, breathwork, and sensual touch. By introducing parts of tantra into their lovemaking, couples may enhance their emotional and physical connection, opening the door to profound levels of pleasure and closeness. Through mindful breathing, focused touch, and reciprocal exploration, couples may create a heightened sense of awareness and present, allowing them to fully immerse themselves in the moment and feel the whole range of sensations.

Similarly, sensory play offers a lively and adventurous method to spice up intimate experiences. This strategy involves engaging the senses through a range of activities, such as blindfolding, temperature play, and sensual massage. By engaging the senses in innovative and surprising ways, partners may heighten arousal and amplify feelings, providing a more immersive and intense sexual encounter. Whether exploring the excitement of anticipation or basking in the pleasure of touch, sensory play enables couples to delve into their sensuous side and appreciate the delights of the present.

Additionally, role-playing scenarios and fantasy fulfilment may lend an element of excitement and freshness to sexual experiences. By stepping into different roles or identities, partners may explore new parts of their sexuality and indulge in their innermost desires. Whether performing a passionate dream or just trying on a new identity, role-playing allows couples to transcend the limits of ordinary life and explore the vast possibilities of their imagination. By embracing fantasy and creativity in the bedroom, couples may add a feeling of excitement and spontaneity into their sex life, keeping the flames of desire burning hot.

Embracing digital platforms and online resources may transform personal relationships by offering access to a variety of information, inspiration, and support. Educational websites, forums, and blogs offer important tools for couples looking to increase their awareness of sexual health, communication, and pleasure enhancement. By accessing these online resources, couples may get useful insights and help on a broad variety of issues, from sexual methods to handling relationship problems, allowing them to create healthier and more rewarding personal interactions.

Virtual communities and relationship applications offer extra options for couples to enrich their personal interactions. These platforms give a forum for users to interact with like-minded persons, exchange experiences, and explore new desires in a safe and friendly setting. Whether seeking counsel, affirmation, or friendship, couples may discover a feeling of community and belonging inside these digital spaces, developing a sense of camaraderie and solidarity in their private journey.

Furthermore, internet therapy and counselling services offer a simple and accessible alternative for couples to address marital difficulties and deepen their emotional connection. Through virtual sessions with qualified specialists, couples may explore communication skills, negotiate issues, and expand their awareness of each other's needs and aspirations. By using the power of technology, couples may obtain the assistance and guidance they need to overcome hurdles and create more rewarding and harmonious relationships, both in and out of the bedroom.

Integrating innovation into intimate interactions encourages couples to embark on a path of sexual discovery, growth, and pleasure. By adopting new technology, techniques, and approaches, couples may expand their relationship, strengthen their connection, and create lasting memories that promote intimacy and happiness for years to come.

Chapter Eight:

Embracing Your Sexual Identity

Discovering who you are sexually is like beginning on a quest to understand oneself better. It's about recognizing and enjoying what makes you unique — your desires, interests, and what makes you feel good. Sometimes, there are emotions of shame or guilt that emerge from inside or from what society expects. But it's crucial to let go of those negative sentiments and appreciate who you actually are. This path also requires recognizing and appreciating the varied ways that people display their sexuality. It's about establishing a safe and inviting atmosphere for everyone to be themselves without judgement or discrimination.

1. Celebrating Individual Preferences and Desires

Celebrating individual preferences and wants in sexuality includes acknowledging and appreciating the distinct tastes and inclinations that each person possesses. It involves a wide range of characteristics, including what turns someone on, what they find delightful, and the precise acts or fantasies they like in sexual experiences.

Firstly, it's essential to realise that everyone's sexual preferences are genuine and deserving of respect, regardless of whether they correspond with cultural standards or expectations. This involves realising that what may be pleasant or entertaining to one person may not be the same for another. For example, some persons may favour certain sorts of sexual activities, positions, or role-play scenarios, while others may have specific kinks or fetishes that offer them pleasure. Celebrating individual choices involves realising that variation is natural and acceptable, and there is no one-size-fits-all approach to sexuality.

Acknowledging the legitimacy of everyone's sexual preferences is vital to creating inclusion and acceptance in society. It's about realising that variation is a natural feature of human sexuality and that there is no single standard for what makes "normal" or "acceptable" wants.

For instance, some people could find enjoyment in more conventional sexual acts like missionary position or oral sex, while others may receive gratification from more unusual practices such as BDSM, role-playing, or exploring fetishes. Each individual's tastes are moulded by a combination of biological, psychological, and cultural influences, making them unique and deserving of respect.

By embracing this variety, we can create a more inclusive and understanding atmosphere where individuals feel encouraged to express themselves genuinely without fear of criticism or stigma. This involves supporting open and non-judgmental discussion about sexual urges and preferences, both inside personal relationships and in larger cultural contexts.

Moreover, honouring individual choices requires confronting cultural norms and expectations that influence what is deemed "normal" or "appropriate" in terms of sexuality. It entails arguing for the rights of individuals to explore and express their wants freely, regardless of whether they adhere to established standards.

By embracing and celebrating the diversity of sexual preferences, we can promote a culture of acceptance, respect, and empowerment, where everyone feels valued and validated in their unique sexual identity.

Moreover, recognizing individual wants includes establishing an environment where individuals feel comfortable and encouraged to explore and express their sexuality openly. This entails reducing stigma, shame, and condemnation surrounding sexual preferences and wants. It's about promoting open and non-judgmental communication with partners, allowing for honest talks about likes, dislikes, limits, and dreams. By developing a culture of acceptance and tolerance, individuals might feel more secure and liberated in expressing their unique sexual identities.

Creating a secure and empowering atmosphere for individuals to explore and express their sexuality honestly is vital for developing overall well-being and contentment. This entails eliminating cultural stigmas and taboos around sexuality and providing spaces where individuals feel free from judgement and shame.

One approach to do this is by establishing open and honest conversation with partners about sexual preferences, desires, and boundaries. By fostering a culture of acceptance and understanding within intimate relationships, individuals can feel more comfortable revealing their deepest needs and dreams without fear of rejection or judgement.

Moreover, it's necessary to combat damaging assumptions and beliefs about sexuality that promote shame and stigma. This might entail encouraging sex-positive attitudes and lobbying for comprehensive sexual education that stresses consent, pleasure, and variety in sexual expression.

Additionally, offering access to supporting services and networks can help individuals feel less alienated and more validated in their sexual identities. This may include online forums, support groups, or therapy services where people may seek help, affirmation, and support in navigating their sexual journey.

Celebrating individual wants means appreciating the diversity of human sexuality and celebrating the intrinsic worth and legitimacy of each person's unique sexual identity. By fostering a culture of acceptance and empowerment, we can create better and more rewarding relationships with ourselves and others.

Additionally, respecting individual choices requires accepting the notion of sexual autonomy and agency. This implies acknowledging that each individual has the freedom to make their own decisions regarding their sexual encounters, free from compulsion, pressure, or condemnation. It's about respecting someone's capacity to agree to the activities they engage in and acknowledging their boundaries and restrictions. By empowering individuals to exercise responsibility over their sexual lives, we build a culture of respect and dignity in sexual encounters.

Embracing the notion of sexual autonomy and agency is vital for building healthy and respectful sexual interactions. It's about acknowledging and honouring each individual's freedom to make educated decisions regarding their own bodies and sexual experiences.

Respecting sexual autonomy involves realising that consent is vital in all sexual relationships. This means securing explicit and enthusiastic agreement from all people involved and respecting their right to say no or withdraw consent at any moment. It's crucial to emphasise communication and actively listen to partners' needs and boundaries to ensure that all interactions are consensual and mutually enjoyable.

Furthermore, valuing sexual liberty entails rejecting any sort of coercion, manipulation, or pressure in sexual relationships. This involves abstaining from using guilt, threats, or emotional manipulation to push someone into engaging in sexual acts against their will. Instead, it's crucial to promote mutual respect, trust, and understanding in all relationships, allowing individuals to feel powerful and in charge of their own sexual experiences.

Promoting sexual autonomy also involves pushing for comprehensive sexual education and access to services that allow individuals to make educated decisions about their sexual health and well-being. By giving accurate information on consent, boundaries, contraception, and STI prevention, we can empower individuals with the knowledge and skills they need to navigate their sexual lives with confidence and autonomy.

Celebrating individual preferences includes building a culture that respects and cherishes each person's freedom to self-determination in their sexual experiences. By fostering sexual autonomy and agency, we may develop healthier, more meaningful relationships centred on trust, respect, and mutual consent.

Overall, recognizing individual tastes and desires in sexuality is about appreciating variety, creating acceptance, and supporting autonomy. By establishing a friendly and inclusive environment where everyone's unique sexual identity is embraced and appreciated, we contribute to a more meaningful and happy sexual experience for all those participating.

2. Overcoming Shame and Guilt Surrounding Sexuality

Overcoming shame and guilt regarding sexuality is a profoundly personal and frequently tough path for many individuals. Shame and guilt can arise from a variety of causes, including society conventions, cultural views, religious teachings, prior experiences, and interpersonal connections. These negative sentiments can emerge in numerous ways, such as feeling humiliated or inadequate about one's wants, experiences, or identity, or experiencing fear of judgement or rejection from others.

One of the first stages in overcoming shame and guilt regarding sexuality is identifying and embracing these sentiments without judgement. It's crucial to know that experiencing shame or guilt about one's sexuality is not unusual and does not make someone fundamentally faulty or undesirable. By admitting these sentiments, individuals may begin to investigate their roots and move towards understanding and treating them.

Acknowledging and embracing emotions of shame or guilt surrounding sexuality is a critical starting point in the road towards healing and self-acceptance. It's crucial to recognize that these sentiments are natural and do not indicate any underlying weakness or deficiency within oneself. Instead of blaming or condemning oneself for having these emotions, it's crucial to approach them with kindness and inquiry.

By accepting these sensations without judgement, individuals may make room for investigation and insight. They can begin to ask themselves questions such as where these sentiments originated from, what societal or cultural messages have affected them, and how these feelings have impacted their views and behaviours. This process of self-reflection helps individuals to acquire insight into the main reasons for their shame and guilt and encourages them to confront these underlying difficulties.

Moreover, expressing and embracing feelings of shame or guilt can help individuals break out from the cycle of self-criticism and self-blame.

Instead of reinforcing negative ideas and beliefs about oneself, individuals might develop a more compassionate and forgiving attitude towards themselves. This shift in viewpoint enables for more self-understanding and self-compassion, establishing the framework for healing and growth.

Acknowledging and embracing emotions of shame or guilt regarding sexuality is a vital step towards recovering one's sense of self-worth and dignity. It helps individuals to tackle these feelings with courage and vulnerability, leading the way for deeper self-awareness, acceptance, and eventually, a more meaningful and honest expression of sexuality.

Seeking support from trusted friends or experts can give vital aid in navigating and overcoming emotions of shame and guilt regarding sexuality. Opening out to friends, family members, or supportive peers about one's experiences and emotions may bring affirmation, empathy, and a sense of connection. Sharing freely and honestly with others can help folks feel less alienated and alone in their challenges, while also giving possibilities for empathy and encouragement.

Moreover, obtaining help from mental health specialists, such as therapists or counsellors, can give specific support and tools for resolving difficulties connected to shame and guilt regarding sexuality. Therapists provide a safe and confidential environment for individuals to address the underlying issues leading to their emotions of shame and guilt, such as prior traumas, cultural pressures, or internalised beliefs. Through therapy, individuals can acquire insight into the fundamental reasons of their issues and learn coping methods for managing and overcoming these challenges.

Therapists may apply numerous therapy tactics and approaches to assist patients negotiate their experiences with shame and guilt regarding sexuality. Cognitive-behavioural therapy (CBT) may be used to uncover and confront negative thinking patterns and beliefs, while mindfulness-based practices can help patients grow self-compassion and acceptance. Additionally, psychoeducation may be offered to assist individuals better understand the social and cultural aspects driving their emotions of shame and guilt.

Seeking help from trustworthy friends, family members, or mental health experts can be crucial in the road towards healing and self-acceptance. By seeking out for help and guidance, individuals may obtain the support, affirmation, and tools they need to manage their experiences with shame and guilt around sexuality, eventually allowing them to recover their sense of self-worth and live honestly.

Challenging societal norms and cultural messaging that lead to emotions of shame and guilt surrounding sexuality is a critical step in developing acceptance and inclusiveness. This process entails challenging and deconstructing inflexible gender norms, heteronormative beliefs, and other damaging stereotypes that perpetuate stigma and judgement. By rejecting these conventions, individuals may encourage a more open and inclusive discussion about sexuality, allowing room for varied experiences and identities to be acknowledged and embraced.

One method to disrupt established norms is by challenging traditional gender roles and expectations that define how individuals should act or express themselves based on their gender. This entails acknowledging that gender is a continuum and that people should be able to explore and express their identity in ways that seem true to them, regardless of cultural expectations. By questioning gender norms, individuals may break free from confining assumptions and embrace a more fluid and inclusive perspective of gender identity and expression.

Additionally, challenging heteronormative norms includes accepting and embracing varied sexual orientations and relationship forms beyond the typical heterosexual paradigm. This implies acknowledging that love and desire come in many forms and that all consensual relationships deserve respect and acknowledgment, regardless of sexual orientation or gender identity. By opposing heteronormativity, individuals may provide space for LGBTQ+ individuals to live freely and truthfully, free from stigma and prejudice.

Advocating for more acceptance and tolerance in talks about sexuality is another crucial component of changing established standards. This entails fostering sex-positive attitudes and recognizing the freedom of individuals to explore and express their sexuality without fear of condemnation or shame. By campaigning for comprehensive sex education, LGBTQ+ rights, and inclusive representation in media and culture, individuals may help create a more welcoming and accepting environment for everyone, regardless of their sexual orientation, gender identity, or relationship choices.

Challenging societal norms and cultural messages that promote shame and guilt surrounding sexuality is vital for developing a more inclusive and welcoming culture. By questioning traditional gender norms, challenging heteronormative beliefs, and pushing for more acceptance and tolerance, individuals may build a culture of acceptance, diversity, and empowerment in which all individuals feel valued, respected, and free to explore their real selves.

Engaging in self-reflection and self-compassion is a critical element of overcoming shame and guilt regarding sexuality. This process entails taking time to think on one's ideas, feelings, and experiences relating to sexuality without judgement or condemnation. It's about embracing the authenticity of one's feelings and experiences, even if they are hard or uncomfortable.

Self-compassion also means treating oneself with care and understanding, much as one would treat a close friend or loved one. This is providing oneself words of encouragement, support, and comfort in times of struggle or suffering. It's about accepting that everyone makes errors and endures periods of difficulty, and that it's alright to be flawed.

Practising forgiveness and acceptance towards oneself is another crucial part of self-compassion. This means letting go of self-blame and self-criticism, and instead, embracing oneself with love and understanding. It's about realising that one's value is not decided by previous deeds or experiences, and that it's never too late to make positive adjustments and improve.

Developing a strong and compassionate relationship with oneself can enable individuals to overcome emotions of shame and guilt regarding sexuality. By growing self-awareness, self-acceptance, and self-compassion, individuals may let go of negative self-judgement and embrace their sexuality with confidence, authenticity, and self-assurance.

Overcoming shame and guilt regarding sexuality is a path that involves patience, self-awareness, and bravery. By understanding and resolving these feelings, getting assistance when required, questioning cultural conventions, and fostering self-compassion, individuals may recover their sexual autonomy and enjoy their sexuality with honesty and pride.

3. Embracing Diversity and Inclusivity in Sexual Expression

Embracing diversity and inclusion in sexual expression is a complicated task that demands a profound grasp of the complexity and subtleties of human sexuality. It entails accepting and appreciating the range of sexual orientations, gender identities, desires, and behaviours that exist throughout society. Below are some crucial factors to consider while examining this issue in further detail:

1. Understanding Sexual Orientation and Gender Identity:
Sexual orientation refers to a person's emotional, romantic, or sexual attraction to others. It comprises identities such as heterosexual, gay, bisexual, pansexual, and asexual, among others. Gender identification, on the other hand, refers to a person's internal perception of their own gender, which may or may not coincide with the sex they were assigned at birth. Embracing variety in sexual expression implies embracing and affirming the legitimacy of all sexual orientations and gender identities.

2. Recognizing Intersectionality:
Human sexuality is impacted by a myriad of elements, including race, ethnicity, culture, religion, handicap, and socioeconomic position, among others. It's crucial to acknowledge that individuals may encounter distinct obstacles and intersections of identity that influence their sexual experiences and expression. Embracing diversity entails recognizing and appreciating these overlapping identities and the manner in which they connect with sexuality.

3. Challenging Stereotypes and Stigma:
Stereotypes, biases, and stigmas around sexuality can create hurdles to acceptance and inclusion for underrepresented groups. Embracing diversity entails confronting these damaging tropes and working for more truthful, affirming depictions of varied sexualities in media, education, and society at large. It's about fostering understanding, respect, and compassion for persons whose sexual identities and experiences differ from the norm.

4. Promoting Inclusivity in Sexual Spaces:
Creating inclusive spaces where individuals of all sexual orientations and gender identities feel welcome and respected is vital for developing

variety in sexual expression. This may entail creating policies and procedures that promote equality and nondiscrimination, offering education and training on LGBTQ+ topics, and actively integrating various views and viewpoints in decision-making processes. It's about establishing settings where everyone feels appreciated, acknowledged, and celebrated for who they are.

5. Supporting Sexual Health and Well-being: Embracing variety in sexual expression also means assuring access to comprehensive sexual health care, education, and resources for all persons, regardless of their sexual orientation or identity. This involves offering inclusive sexual health treatments that meet the special needs and concerns of LGBTQ+ persons, as well as supporting sex-positive, nonjudgmental approaches to sexual education and health promotion. It's about enabling individuals to make educated decisions about their sexual health and well-being and giving support and tools to assist them navigate their sexual journeys.

Supporting variety and tolerance in sexual expression demands a dedication to knowledge, acceptance, and appreciation of the whole spectrum of human sexuality. It's about building a society where everyone feels seen, heard, and respected for their individual sexual identities and experiences, and where variety is cherished as a source of strength and richness in our collective human experience.

Chapters Nine:

Sustaining Passion in Long-Term Relationships

Sustaining Passion in Long-Term Relationships is like fostering a magnificent garden of love that blossoms and flourishes over time. It's about keeping the enchantment alive even after years of being together, like putting sprinkles of excitement to your favourite dish.

In this last chapter, we'll walk through the magical forest of love, uncovering secret routes and hidden treasures to keep your relationship alive and blooming. We'll unearth the power of tiny actions, like sowing seeds of affection through embraces and charming messages, then nurturing them with open communication and understanding.

Furthermore, we'll establish bridges of closeness with rituals and routines, building comfortable nests of togetherness where you can snuggle up and share your dreams. Whether it's dancing beneath the stars or whispering secrets in the moonlight, these rituals form the lifeblood of your relationship, keeping it healthy and lively.

And let's not forget the thrill of physical connection - the delicate caress of a hand, the warmth of an embrace, the spark of a kiss. Like parts of a jigsaw, these moments fit together to produce a masterpiece of passion and pleasure.

So, let's go on this amazing trip together, where love has no limitations, and every moment is an adventure waiting to be shared. With a sprinkling of imagination and a dash of spontaneity, we'll keep the fires of passion burning hot, lighting up the way to eternal love and happiness.

1. Strategies for Keeping the Spark Alive After Years Together

Keeping the spark alive in a long-term relationship is like tending to a fire — it takes attention and care to remain blazing bright. Here are some basic techniques to keep the spark of love alive even after many years together:

1. Quality Time Together: Quality time together is about prioritising each other in your hectic life. It means setting aside specific time to focus exclusively on your spouse, free from distractions like work, screens, or other responsibilities. This time may be spent engaging in activities that you

both like and that allow you to connect on a deeper level. Whether it's having a profound discussion over dinner, discovering a new pastime together, or simply enjoying each other's company in quiet, the goal is to be totally present and responsive to each other's needs. By developing these times of connection, you may build your bond and keep the spark alive in your relationship.

2. Surprise and Variation: Surprises and variation play a significant part in keeping the flame alive in a long-term relationship. Over time, routines can become dull, and couples may find themselves trapped in a rut. Injecting shocks and variety into the relationship helps break this monotony and keeps the excitement alive.

Surprises may come in various ways, from organising surprise dates or trips to impulsively attempting new hobbies together. It's about breaking the routine and doing something out of the ordinary that takes your partner off guard and brings a grin to their face. It might be as easy as dropping a love note in their lunchbox or planning a surprise picnic in the park.

Variety is equally vital. Trying new activities together not only brings excitement but also helps couples to learn and develop together. Whether it's pursuing a new pastime, visiting a new area, or trying a new restaurant, venturing out of your comfort zone together deepens your friendship and generates shared experiences.

These surprises and new experiences show your lover that you're interested in keeping the relationship fresh and intriguing. It displays intelligence, spontaneity, and a desire to invest work into developing the connection. By embracing surprises and variation, couples may renew the passion and keep the flame alive in their long-term relationship.

3. Communication and Connection: Communication and connection are the core of a successful and lasting relationship. In the rush and bustle of daily life, it's easy for couples to drift apart or take each other for granted. That's why creating time for open and honest conversation is vital.

Sit down with your spouse regularly and talk about your feelings, desires, and dreams. Share what's on your mind and listen intently when they talk. Communication isn't only about talking; it's also about attentively listening to your partner's ideas and emotions without judgement.

Expressing oneself truthfully is crucial. Don't be reluctant to discuss your vulnerabilities, worries, and hopes with your spouse. Opening out in this way creates trust and improves the emotional connection between you.

Remember, communication isn't just about talking about major problems; it's also about sharing the simple things that make up your day-to-day life. Whether it's talking about your favourite TV show or reminiscing about a hilarious story, these moments of connection build your bond and keep the flame alive.

By prioritising communication and connection, you guarantee that both you and your spouse feel heard, understood, and appreciated in the relationship. This provides the framework for a solid, enduring connection focused on trust, respect, and love.

4. Physical Affection: Physical affection is a strong technique to cultivate closeness and keep the flame alive in your relationship. Simple actions like holding hands, embracing, kissing,

and snuggling may speak volumes and enhance the relationship between you and your spouse.

Make it a practice to exhibit affection consistently, whether it's a short kiss goodbye in the morning or a strong embrace when you rejoin at the end of the day. Physical contact generates feel-good chemicals like oxytocin and dopamine, which boost sensations of love, security, and contentment.

Don't underestimate the power of non-verbal communication. A delicate touch on the arm or a lengthy hug shows love and support without the need for words. These simple gestures of physical kindness establish a sense of intimacy and deepen your emotional connection.

Incorporating physical touch into your everyday routine keeps the connection alive and reminds you both of the love and affection you share. It's a simple yet significant method to nourish your connection and guarantee that the spark continues to burn brightly for years to come.

5. Shared Goals and ambitions: Sharing goals and ambitions with your spouse is a strong method to build your bond and keep your relationship healthy. When you both have

common aims to strive towards, it promotes a sense of togetherness and collaboration.

Sit down together and discuss your ambitions, both individually and as a pair. Whether it's saving up for a dream vacation, purchasing a house, or learning a new skill together, having shared objectives gives you something to look forward to and strive towards as a team.

Working towards mutual objectives not only enriches your relationship but also generates lasting memories and experiences that you can appreciate together. It develops a sense of cooperation and collaboration, reminding you both that you're in this path of life together.

Make sure to recognize milestones and victories along the road, no matter how minor. Acknowledge each other's efforts and assist each other through hardships. Sharing goals and ambitions not only enhances your connection but also keeps the excitement and passion alive in your relationship.

6. Maintain Independence: Maintaining independence within your relationship is vital for keeping the spark alive and ensuring that both partners continue to grow separately. While

spending time together is crucial, it's also important to foster your own interests and hobbies.

Encourage each other to pursue hobbies that offer joy and contentment, whether it's a single pastime like painting or joining a sports team with buddies. Having time apart helps you to preserve a feeling of independence and self-discovery, which in turn enhances your partnership.

Respecting each other's desire for space and independence produces a healthy dynamic where both parties feel supported and respected. It also eliminates emotions of suffocation or anger that might emerge when boundaries are not maintained.

By retaining independence and supporting each other's personal progress, you not only enhance your bond as a pair but also ensure that your partnership remains dynamic and enjoyable in the long run.

By adopting these easy tactics into your relationship, you can keep the flame alive and develop a love that continues to grow stronger with each passing year.

2. Building Rituals and Routines that Support Intimacy

Building rituals and routines that encourage intimacy requires adopting regular habits and activities that bring you closer together as a pair. These rituals help strengthen your partnership, boost communication, and deepen emotional connection. Here are some easy approaches to design such rituals:

1. Daily Check-Ins: Daily check-ins are like tiny discussions you have with your spouse every day to catch up on what's going on in each other's life. It's a moment to discuss how you're feeling, chat about what happened throughout the day, and listen to your partner's opinions too. You may do this while eating breakfast together, taking a walk, or right before going to sleep. It's a method to remain connected and understand each other better.

2. Weekly Date Nights: Weekly date nights are special evenings set aside solely for the two of you to spend quality time together. It's like having a tiny celebration of your love once a week. You may go out for a lovely dinner, watch a movie at home cuddling up on the sofa, or try something new together like preparing a new

recipe or taking a dancing class. The key thing is to focus on each other and have fun without any distractions.

3. Shared Hobbies or Interests: Shared hobbies or interests are something you both love doing together. It may be anything from preparing excellent food, growing a garden, or even learning how to dance salsa. By enjoying these activities, you're not only having fun together but also expanding your friendship and generating lasting memories. Plus, it offers you something to look forward to and helps you grow closer as a pair.

4. Physical Contact: Physical contact is a vital aspect of creating closeness in a relationship. It might be as basic as giving each other a hug or a kiss, holding hands, or snuggling on the couch. These tiny acts let you feel connected and appreciated, even in the midst of your hectic life. So, be sure to add physical affection into your everyday routine to enhance your relationship and keep the flame alive.

5. Bedtime Rituals: Bedtime rituals can be a great way to relax down and connect with your mate before sleep. You could cuddle up together, exchange anecdotes from your day, or express

thanks for each other's presence. These moments of connection help build your bond and guarantee you both feel loved and valued as you go off to sleep. So, make it a habit to develop nighttime rituals that encourage intimacy and relaxation, setting the mood for a quiet night and a deep connection with your spouse.

6. Expressing Thankfulness: Expressing thankfulness is a wonderful approach to improve your connection. Take time each day to acknowledge your partner's presence and contributions. You may say thank you for the tiny things they do, put love notes about the house, or surprise them with meaningful gestures. Cultivating a culture of thankfulness not only enhances your link but also develops a pleasant and supportive relationship dynamic. So, make expressing thankfulness a regular part of your routine, and watch your relationship bloom with appreciation and love.

3. Rediscovering the Joy of Physical Connection

Rediscovering the delight of physical connection in your relationship entails reconnecting with each other on a bodily level and reigniting the flame of intimacy. Here are several basic methods to achieve that:

1. Prioritise Touch: Prioritising touch involves purposefully bringing physical affection into your everyday routine with your spouse. This might be holding hands while walking, offering embraces when you meet each other or say goodbye, or snuggling on the sofa while watching TV or reading together.

These small acts of physical contact have huge consequences on your relationship. When you contact, your body releases oxytocin, frequently termed the "love hormone," which fosters emotions of connection, trust, and intimacy. Oxytocin also helps relieve tension and anxiety, generating a sense of calm and security between lovers.

Regular physical touch increases the emotional relationship between you and your spouse, expanding your connection and increasing emotions of intimacy and affection. It's a method to show love, warmth, and support without words, establishing a sense of comfort and safety inside the partnership.

By prioritising touch in your relationship, you show your spouse that you appreciate their presence and crave physical connection with them. It's a simple yet effective approach to nourish and preserve the emotional and physical connection that keeps your relationship healthy and happy.

2. Intimate Gestures: Intimate gestures are those subtle, intentional behaviours that communicate affection and desire for your companion. These gestures might be spontaneous or planned, but their objective is to generate moments of intimacy and connection between you and your spouse.

One example of an intimate gesture is to surprise your lover with a back rub after a long day at work. This implies that you care about their well-being and wish to give them physical comfort and relaxation. Another gesture may be kissing your spouse unexpectedly, whether it's a brief peck on the cheek or a passionate kiss that stays a bit longer. These unexpected gestures of affection may brighten your partner's day and remind them of your love and desire for them.

Giving your lover a lengthy embrace is another personal act that may revive the physical connection between you. Hugs release oxytocin, the "love hormone," which boosts emotions of bonding and connection. By hugging your lover warmly and holding them close, you transmit your devotion and create a sense of security and connection.

Intimate gestures don't have to be huge or complex; it's the thinking and meaning behind them that count most. Whether it's a simple touch, a loving gaze, or a sensitive hug, these gestures express your love, desire, and dedication to your spouse, increasing the physical connection between you and expanding your bond.

3. Explore Sensuality: Exploring sensuality means adopting an intentional and focused approach to connecting with your partner's body and experiencing pleasure together. It's about slowing down, being present in the moment, and exploring one other's bodies with curiosity and openness.

One method to explore sensuality is to engage in activities that heighten your senses and improve bodily awareness. This might entail blindfolded touch, when one person is blindfolded while the other employs varied textures or sensations to excite their partner's body. Experimenting with temperature play, such as employing ice cubes or heated oils during massage, may help boost sensory awareness and arousal.

Another facet of exploring sensuality is trying different techniques and positions to determine what feels best for you and your partner. This might entail experimenting with different sorts of touch, pressure, and rhythm to determine what generates the most pleasure. Communication is crucial throughout this inquiry, as it allows you to provide and accept feedback, alter your approach, and strengthen your relationship.

Exploring sensuality isn't only about physical contact; it also entails activating your other senses, such as sight, smell, and sound, to enrich the total experience. Setting the setting with soft lighting, fragrant candles, and relaxing music may create a sensuous ambiance that heightens arousal and closeness.

Ultimately, experiencing sensuality is about honouring the beauty and pleasure of the human body and creating moments of profound connection and intimacy with your partner. By taking the time to explore each other's body and sensations, you may improve your physical connection, boost sexual pleasure, and build your relationship as a couple.

4. Communicate Openly: Open communication is vital for regaining the delight of physical connection in your relationship. By freely sharing your desires, dreams, and preferences with your partner, you create a safe and supportive atmosphere where you may explore new methods of connecting physically.

Start by beginning an honest and non-judgmental conversation with your spouse about your ideas and feelings around physical intimacy. Share what you appreciate and what you would want to try together, and urge your spouse to do the same. This open discussion helps you to better understand each other's wants and offer possibilities for mutual discovery and enjoyment.

During these interactions, be careful to listen closely to your partner's comments and affirm their thoughts and desires. Avoid judgement or criticism, and instead, focus on creating empathy and understanding. Remember that everyone has various comfort levels and boundaries when it comes to physical intimacy, so it's crucial to accept and honour your partner's preferences.

As you talk freely with your spouse about your physical wants and desires, be prepared to compromise and explore new experiences together. Be open to attempting new things and moving beyond your comfort zone, recognizing that development and connection frequently occur when you push your boundaries together.

By discussing freely and honestly with your spouse about your wishes and preferences, you develop a foundation of trust and intimacy that helps you to rediscover the joy of physical connection in your relationship. Embrace vulnerability, be attentive to your partner's needs, and relish the process of exploration and discovery together.

5. Try New activities: Trying new activities together may provide a feeling of adventure and excitement to your physical connection. By exploring new activities or experiences together,

you create opportunities to bond, connect, and rediscover the delight of physical connection.

Consider preparing a variety of activities that appeal to both you and your partner's hobbies and preferences. Whether it's getting a couples massage to wallow in relaxation and intimacy, taking a dancing class to appreciate movement and connection, or travelling on a romantic holiday to discover new places and make lasting memories, the goal is to venture outside of your comfort zone and do something new together.

When exploring new things, focus on being present in the moment and enjoying the experience together. Allow yourselves to let go of any expectations or demands and simply immerse yourselves in the shared experience. Whether you're learning a new dance step, touring a new city, or eating a new cuisine, enjoy the journey and appreciate the chance to connect with each other in a meaningful way.

As you start on new adventures together, keep communication open and honest. Share your ideas, feelings, and experiences with each other, and be attentive to your partner's criticism and wants. By actively engaging in new activities and experiences together, you not only increase your physical connection but also strengthen your bond and create lasting memories that you may enjoy together for years to come.

6. Make Time for Intimacy: Making time for intimacy is vital for fostering the physical connection between you and your spouse. Amidst the rush and bustle of daily life, it's crucial to set out devoted time to prioritise each other and reignite the joy of physical connection.

Consider organising frequent date nights or personal evenings at home when you can focus entirely on each other without interruptions. Choose activities that foster closeness and connection, whether it's preparing a romantic dinner together, taking a candlelight bath, or simply snuggling on the sofa while watching a movie. The objective is to establish a location where you can relax, unwind, and enjoy each other's company in a meaningful way.

When arranging private moments together, be diligent about establishing a romantic ambiance that enhances the mood and invites closeness. Light candles, play calm music, and set aside any distractions like phones or electrical gadgets. By establishing a sensory-rich atmosphere, you may heighten the sensation of intimacy and enhance your connection with your spouse.

During your personal moments together, focus on being present in the moment and responsive to each other's wants and wishes. Take the time to explore each other's bodies, convey affection, and talk honestly about what feels good and what you both appreciate. By emphasising intimacy and making it a regular part of your routine, you can enhance your physical connection and keep the flame alive in your relationship.

Conclusion:

As we enter middle age, our perspective on sexuality might undergo a metamorphosis. It's a moment to honour our bodies and passions, recognizing the power they possess. Instead of perceiving it as a decline, we can regard this moment as a chance for research and discovery.

Middle age carries with it a variety of experiences and knowledge. We may utilise this information to explore new elements of closeness and pleasure. Rather than feeling restricted by cultural norms, we should feel liberated to accept our impulses without guilt or criticism.

Exploring our sexuality in middle age entails being open to new experiences and activities. It's about approaching sex with a feeling of wonder and enthusiasm, trying new techniques, and discovering what offers us joy and fulfilment. It's also about strengthening emotional ties with our partners, expressing our thoughts and feelings, and creating a space where we can be completely ourselves.

But sexuality in middle age isn't only about bodily pleasure. It's also about emotional closeness and connection. It's about sustaining our connections and developing a sense of intimacy that goes beyond the physical. By accepting change and being open to new opportunities, we may build a satisfying and passionate second chapter in our lives.

As we approach midlife, it's crucial to appreciate and enjoy the power and potential that come with our sexuality at this era. Instead of perceiving it as a time of decline, we should appreciate the particular power and promise that midlife sexuality brings.

At this level, we have a greater grasp of ourselves and our body. We've experienced experiences that have influenced our desires and preferences, and we may utilise this information to seek new routes of pleasure and fulfilment. Midlife sexuality is about embracing the changes in our bodies and our desires, and realising that they may lead to new and exciting experiences.

It's also a moment to celebrate the confidence and self-assurance that comes with age. We no longer feel the need to conform to cultural expectations or adhere to conventional ideals of beauty. Instead, we may embrace our bodies and our wants with a sense of pride and confidence.

Midlife sexuality is about acknowledging that our wants and needs may alter over time, and that's entirely acceptable. It's about being open to new experiences and possibilities, and embracing the opportunities for development and discovery that come with age.

Midlife sexuality is a celebration of the diversity and complexity of our sexual experiences, and the promise for continuous development and satisfaction as we travel through life.

Encouraging a feeling of inquiry, exploration, and fun in our sexual life may offer excitement, delight, and happiness. Instead of clinging to routine or being scared to explore new things, we should adopt an attitude of openness and curiosity when it comes to our sexuality.

Curiosity permits us to approach our sexual encounters with a feeling of wonder and curiosity. It involves being willing to ask questions, explore new ideas, and learn more about ourselves and our partners. By being interested, we may learn what provides us joy, what turns us on, and what excites us, leading to deeper relationships and more meaningful experiences.

Exploration means moving outside of our comfort zones and attempting new things. It implies being open to new experiences, whether it's experimenting with different positions, trying out new fantasies, or exploring new techniques. Through investigation, we can find new sources of pleasure and excitement, and broaden our awareness of what is possible in our sexual life.

Playfulness provides an element of joy and lightheartedness to our sexual relationships. It entails being willing to joke, be foolish, and not take oneself too seriously. By approaching sex with a lighthearted attitude, we may lessen pressure and anxiety, and create a more comfortable and joyful setting. Playfulness encourages us to be creative, spontaneous, and adventurous in the bedroom, resulting in memorable and rewarding encounters for both partners.

Overall, encouraging curiosity, inquiry, and fun into our sexual life may lead to better fulfilment, closeness, and connection. It helps us to embrace the whole range of our needs and dreams, and to approach sex with a sense of pleasure and delight.

Embracing the concept that our sexual journey doesn't have an expiry date gives up a world of possibilities for enjoying pleasure and closeness later in life. Instead of assuming that our finest sexual experiences are behind us, we can embrace our older years as an opportunity to explore new frontiers and discover new parts of our sexuality.

It's about acknowledging that as we age, our bodies and preferences may change, but that doesn't mean we have to settle for less. Throughout fact, many people discover that their sexual encounters throughout midlife and beyond can be even more rewarding and pleasurable than when they were younger.

By adopting the concept of a "steamy second chapter," we may approach our sexual lives with a feeling of enthusiasm and expectation. We may explore new imaginations, try out different tactics, and enhance our ties with our partners. Whether it's reigniting the fire in a long-term partnership or exploring new connections later in life, there are countless opportunities for enjoying pleasure and intimacy.

It's also about letting go of cultural standards and embracing our own individual needs and preferences. Instead of feeling bound by age or societal expectations, we should embrace our latter years as a chance to be true to ourselves and pursue what offers us joy and contentment.

Ultimately, embracing the boundless possibilities of a sizzling second chapter involves approaching our sexual life with an open mind and a spirit of adventure. It's about accepting change, embracing our bodies, and embracing the path of sexual exploration and discovery at every stage of life.